■ Adventur

IDAHO'S SAWTOOTH COUNTRY

by
Lynne Stone

THE
MOUNTAINEERS

To Louis Stur and Loren Adkins—two gentle men of Idaho's mountains

The Mountaineers: Organized 1906 "*... to explore, study, preserve, and enjoy the natural beauty of the Northwest.*

First printing 1990, second printing 1993, third printing 1995, fourth printing 1998

Published by The Mountaineers, 1001 S.W. Klickitat Way, Suite 201
   Seattle, Washington 98134
Manufactured in the United States of America

Edited by Teresa Danielson
Maps by Evelyn Backman Phillips
Cover photographs: Ants Basin, by Joseph Poché. Inset: Hindman Lake
   Road near Cabin Creek Peak, by Lynne Stone.
All photographs by Lynne Stone except as noted: p. 82 by Ernest Day; pp. 117
   and 169 by Christine Jensen; p. 152 by Carol Monteverde; and p. 208 by Scott
   Phillips.
Cover design by Constance Bollen
Book design and layout by Bridget Culligan

Library of Congress Cataloging in Publication Data
Stone, Lynne, 1947-
   Adventures in Idaho's Sawtooth Country / Lynne Stone.
      p.   cm.
   Includes bibliographical references.
   ISBN 0-89886-192-6
   1. Hiking—Idaho—Guide-books.   2. All terrain cycling—Idaho—Guide-books.   3. Hiking—Idaho—Sawtooth National Recreation Area—Guide-books.   4. All terrain cycling—Idaho—Sawtooth National Recreation Area—Guide-books.   5. Idaho—Description and travel—1981-   —Guide-books.
5. Idaho—Description and travel—1981-   —Guide-books.   [1. Sawtooth National Recreation Area (Idaho)—Guide-books.]   I. Title.   II. Title: Idaho's Sawtooth Country.
GV199.42.I2S76   1990
917.96—dc20   90-5669
                                                                                CIP

■ Contents ■

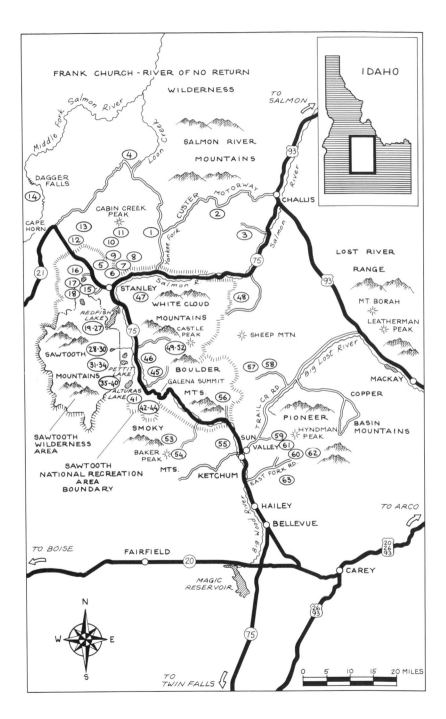

GALENA TO PIONEER MOUNTAINS 167

MAP SYMBOLS

▬▬▬ PAVED ROAD		›‹	MOUNTAIN PASS
═══ UNPAVED ROAD		☀	MOUNTAIN PEAK
==== JEEP TRAIL		○	U.S. HIGHWAY
•••••••• TRAIL		⬭	STATE HIGHWAY
••••••••• TRAIL DESCRIBED IN TRIP		▭	FOREST SERVICE ROAD
••••••••• PRIMITIVE TRAIL		★	STARTING POINT
‖‖‖‖‖ WILDERNESS BOUNDARY		➡	DIRECTION OF TRIP
⌒⌒ RIVER / CREEK		▲	CAMPGROUND (CG)
🌲 FOREST		⌂	RANGER STATION
⚘ MARSH		▫	BUILDING OR CABIN
		✕	MINE

Acknowledgments

The support and encouragement of my family and friends, and the assistance of many others, have enabled me to see this book to completion. I am especially grateful to my mother, Ruth Potter, and brother, Gail Potter, of Condon, Oregon. My son, Bryan, 12, has shared in the exploring, gamely endured more than a few misadventures, and provided the trout for our campfire meals.

Two friends, Pat Ford and Christine Jensen, have been unwavering in their help and spirit of adventure. I cannot thank them enough.

I also want to recognize the zeal and patience of my other biking, hiking, and scrambling companions: Dave Duhaime, Scott Phillips, Mark Klingerman, Denise Jackson, and Ed Cannady. I am grateful to Evelyn Backman Phillips for drawing the book's maps; Tim Crawford for the use of his darkroom; Carol Monteverde for the lessons on printing black-and-white photographs; and George Klingelhofer for the use of his copying machine and cassette recorder.

Many people have kindly answered inquiries or provided other assistance. They include Loren Adkins, Andy Hennig, Andy Munter, Randy Hess, Bob Rosso, and posthumously, Louis Stur and Martin Pollock.

Government personnel have cheerfully supplied information and reviewed the text. My gratitude goes to Gary Gadwa, Idaho Department of Fish and Game; Jay Dorr, Lynn Burton, Jenny Carson, Jeff Jones, Steve Lipus, Ken Britton, Mose Shrum, Art Selin, Butch Harper, John Borton, and Paul Bryant of the Sawtooth Forest Service; and Marion McDaniel and Roberta Green of the Challis Forest Service. Other individuals, too many to list, have also been helpful. Thank you.

I've also appreciated the courteous service of many Ketchum businesses, including F-Stop, Jane's Paper Place, Photographics, Wood River Compu-Print, and the friendly crew at our Ketchum Post Office.

■ Introduction ■

Sawtooth Country

No exact boundaries define Sawtooth Country, but the heart is the 2.1-million-acre Sawtooth National Forest in central Idaho. The jagged spires of the Sawtooth Mountains, with the winding ribbon of the Salmon River at their feet, are postcard material. Idahoans match up the towering 'tooths to any scene in the west.

Five mountain ranges are near the Sawtooths. The Salmon River Mountains lie north. To the east are the White Cloud, Boulder, and Pioneer ranges. The Smoky Mountains lie south. While most of these ranges are in the Sawtooth Forest, some parts are within the neighboring Challis Forest.

This book has destinations in all six ranges. No attempt is made to list every trail or access point. Instead, the day-long (or shorter) trips originate near three interconnected recreation communities: Stanley, Ketchum, and Sun Valley. The outings span from the Cape Horn area west of Stanley to the Pioneer Mountains east of Ketchum, north to the Loon Creek–Beaver Creek Road in the Frank Church–River of No Return Wilderness, and south to the headwaters of the Salmon River.

TOWNS

Stanley is a tiny settlement (population 99) set between the Sawtooth Mountains and the Salmon River, the "River of No Return." Dirt streets and rustic log buildings characterize this small outpost, which hums all summer with hikers, fishermen, family car-campers, and river runners. Stanley is 120 miles northeast of Boise via Highway 21, 120 miles south of Salmon on Highway 75, and 63 miles northwest of Ketchum and Sun Valley on Highway 75.

Ketchum was a quiet mining and ranching town until Sun Valley Resort was built a mile up the road by Union Pacific Railroad in 1936. Today, Ketchum (population 3,280) and Sun Valley (population 660) are bustling cosmopolitan islands in a mountain wonderland. Hardy residents may like the snow and skiing, but it's really the fabulous summers that keep 'em here. (Ask them!) Ketchum, Sun Valley, and two other communities, Hailey (population 2,920) and Bellevue (population 1,500), lie in the Wood River Valley.

Ketchum and Sun Valley are 160 miles northeast of Boise (using Highway 20 through Fairfield), 80 miles north of Twin Falls on Highway 75, and 155 miles west of Idaho Falls.

The 70-minute drive between Ketchum and Stanley on Highway 75 is an exhilarating introduction to the mountain and valley country explored in this book. Halfway between the two towns is Galena Summit (elevation 8,701 feet)

Bluff in East Fork of Nip and Tuck Creek

and Galena Overlook—one of Idaho's most recommended picture-taking sites. From the viewpoint the Sawtooth Mountains rake the western horizon; the Sawtooth Valley and the canyon of the Salmon River headwaters spread below.

Between Ketchum and Stanley are gas and groceries at North Fork, Smiley Creek, Beaver Creek, Obsidian, and Redfish Lake Lodge. Sunbeam Village, downriver from Stanley, also has gas and food.

SAWTOOTH NATIONAL RECREATION AREA

A proposed open-pit molybdenum mine at 11,815-foot Castle Peak in the White Cloud Mountains set off one of Idaho's fiercest conservation battles in the 1960s. It helped lead to creation of the Sawtooth National Recreation Area (SNRA) by Congress in 1972 and propelled a new, more environmentally concerned governor, Cecil Andrus, to the Idaho statehouse.

Castle Peak's domain escaped demolition, and 756,000 acres in the Sawtooth, Challis, and Boise forests were designated for "recreation first" management. Mining, logging, and grazing are still allowed, but only if they do not "substantially impair" the "natural, scenic, historic, pastoral, and fish and wildlife values" of the SNRA. (The interpretation of substantial impairment is often hotly debated.)

Before 1972, subdivision of private land in the Sawtooth Valley threatened long-treasured views of the Sawtooths and White Clouds. The SNRA prevented that destruction, too. Eventually some 2,000 lots were acquired and returned to range land. There are still 22,200 acres of private property within the SNRA, most of it used for grazing. Many scenic easements have been acquired to guarantee the land remains undeveloped.

The major debate in 1972 was not whether to protect Sawtooth Country, but how. A national park and national recreation area were the competing proposals; the latter won out. Existing management allows hunting, firewood gathering, small post and pole timber sales, grazing on public land, unlimited hiking, and abundant unrestricted camping. (Within the SNRA, the communities of Stanley, Obsidian, and Sawtooth City operate as independent municipalities and are governed by different building and zoning regulations.)

Despite predictable, and sometimes justified, grumblings, the SNRA is working. An indication that the original goals are largely being met is the reaction of Brock Evans, vice-president of the National Audubon Society, when he returned to Idaho after a long absence. He told a gathering of conservationists at Redfish Lake Lodge in 1986 that "this [Sawtooth Country] is the only place I've been in the last 10 years that looks better than when I left a decade ago."

MOUNTAIN RANGES

All six Sawtooth Country mountain ranges share basic features. This region of Idaho is on the northern edge of the Great Basin desert. That, along with high altitude and moderate snowfall and rainfall, makes for a semiarid climate. Lodgepole pine covers most north-facing slopes while sagebrush dominates southern hillsides. Higher slopes have subalpine fir, whitebark pine, and limber pine. Douglas fir, Englemann spruce, and ponderosa pine are less abundant. Groves of quaking aspen are common. Black cottonwood trees grow along streams and rivers.

Sawtooth Mountains. The range is part of a large geological formation called the Idaho Batholith (consisting of gray-colored granite) and the smaller Sawtooth Batholith (pink granite). Glacial ice was the master sculptor of these sharp peaks and their cirques. U-shaped glaciated valleys with lateral and terminal moraines spread out below. Thompson Peak (10,751 feet) is the Sawtooth's tallest. Most of the range's 18-mile width and 32-mile length is in the 217,000-acre Sawtooth Wilderness. The Sawtooths are renowned for lakes—close to 200—some with large and plentiful fish. The four largest lakes—Redfish, Stanley, Alturas, and Pettit—are favorites for car camping, boating, and starting points for wilderness hikes.

White Cloud Mountains. East across the Sawtooth Valley lie the White Cloud peaks, much less visible from Highway 75 than their 'toothed neighbors. Starched, soaring summits in the heart of the range are quartzite: a light-colored, metamorphosed sandstone. Often clouds and rock blend as one. Castle Peak (11,815 feet) dominates the range. In width and length the White Clouds are similar to the Sawtooths. Trout fishing is usually productive in many of the 125 backcountry lakes.

Boulder Mountains. Adjoining the White Clouds to the south-southeast and of the same ecosystem are the Boulders, a rough-and-tumble haven of rock and goats. The Boulders are about half the size of the Sawtooths or White Clouds and form the dramatic northern skyline seen from Highway 75 between Ketchum and Galena Summit. There are a few lakes but plenty of solitude. From Ketchum the Boulders are just minutes away, offering valley walks or isolated scrambles onto cloud-swept summits. Ryan Peak (11,714 feet) is the highest and one of five named mountains over 11,000 feet.

Together, the Boulder and White Cloud mountains form the largest remaining unroaded, unprotected (by wilderness status) tract of National Forest land in the lower 48 states—close to one-half million acres.

Smoky Mountains. The Smokys are synonymous with wildlife—especially deer and elk. Terrain is more wooded and rounded than the Boulders and White Clouds or the adjoining Sawtooths, although several peaks rise over 10,000 feet, including the Smokys' highest, Silver Peak (10,441 feet). The Smokys are 40 miles long and 15 to 20 miles wide. One of Idaho's rarest animals, the wolverine, survives in the range. Lakes number a scant two dozen, some with fish. Sun Valley's famous ski runs on 9,151-foot Bald Mountain lie on the eastern edge of the Smokys.

Pioneer Mountains. The sun that named Sun Valley rises over the Pioneer Mountains, followed in evening by a fluorescent moon. The Pioneers are close to Ketchum and Sun Valley, making it a popular hiking area. Trips in this book are on the range's western side. Lower canyons are stream-cut, V-shaped with glaciated basins and narrow, ragged, ice-carved ridges above. There are about three dozen lakes, most with fish. The Pioneers are a compact 12-by-20 miles.

The trail to Pioneer Cabin is the most used (more than 3,000 visitors per season) in the Sawtooth Forest. From the cabin the panorama of alpine summits, including Hyndman Peak at 12,009 feet, is rated a 10-plus.

Salmon River Mountains. North of Stanley lie the Salmon River Mountains, within whose foothills are many of the bicycling trips in this book. Farther north these mountains are designated the Frank Church–River of No Return Wilderness and become an undulating mass of high plateaus, deep canyons, thickly vegetated creek bottoms, and long slopes of sage or timber. *Adventures in Idaho's Sawtooth Country* takes you on a spectacular mountain bicycle ride through the southern edge of the wilderness on the Loon Creek–Beaver Creek Road.

HISTORY

Alexander Ross, British explorer and beaver hunter, climbed to a summit in the Boulder Mountains on September 18, 1824, and looked upon the Sawtooth Valley and the jagged peaks beyond.

"The view we had enjoyed repaid us well for our troubles," said Ross. Ross and his party of trappers saw few beaver, but were the first white men to see the Sawtooth Valley and the skyline that resembled the teeth of a saw beyond. A historical sign on the east side of Galena Summit recognizes Ross's explorations.

Since long before the time of the Ross party, Sheepeater Indians inhabited the area. The Salmon River teemed with salmon, which the Indians caught and dried for winter. The Sheepeaters also hunted elk, deer, antelope, and mountain sheep.

Miners came to Sawtooth land in the 1860s and sought gold in historical Sheepeater hunting and fishing grounds. By 1879, following skirmishes between the Indians and white men, and a confrontation called the Sheepeater War, the Indians were taken from their homeland to reservations.

The 1870s and 1880s were the time of the Sawtooth gold and silver rush. Boom towns sprung up at Sawtooth City, Vienna, Custer, Oro Grande, Ivers, Galena, Ketchum (then called Leadville), Hailey, and others.

Toward the end of the mining era another influx occurred—the first sheep bands were brought from southern Idaho to summer pasture in the high country. Sheep numbers grew and by 1907 there were 364,000 head on the land. Creation of the Sawtooth Forest in 1908 brought needed regulation of livestock. Today 50,000 sheep graze on the northern part of the forest.

The first permanent homesteaders came near the turn of the century. They faced short summer growing seasons and bitterly cold winters. Their names, along with those of explorers, miners, and sheepmen, were given to many Sawtooth peaks and valley streams.

At present, Sawtooth Country is a blend of ranching, a little mining, and most notably, an economy thriving on outdoor recreation made possible by vast tracts of unspoiled public land. Since the establishment of Sun Valley Resort in 1939 brought the outside world's attention to the mountains of north-central Idaho, residents have shared with a host of visitors the superb skiing in winter and the camping, fishing, hiking, backpacking, river running, and other outdoor pursuits in summer.

WILDLIFE

Look for wildlife in early morning or evening hours along streams, meadows, and the edge of timber. You'll often see mule deer and, less frequently, Rocky Mountain elk. Sharp-eyed observers may see Rocky Mountain goats (many transplanted from Olympic National Park) on high ridges while in the backcountry or from roads with the aid of binoculars or spotting scope. Bighorn sheep live in the White Clouds, but they are seldom seen along maintained trails. Goats stay on the crags year-round, while the bighorns winter lower, many near the East Fork of the Salmon River.

A small number of moose inhabit the willows and forests in the North Fork of the Big Lost River (over Trail Creek Summit from Ketchum and Sun Valley). Antelope are summer visitors to upper Sawtooth Valley fields. Coyotes are common, and you may also see red foxes. Smaller animals include the chattery pine squirrel, yellow pine chipmunk, and golden-mantled ground squirrel. Another small mammal, usually seen at dusk, is the mosquito-devouring bat.

Over 100 species of birds are listed in the Sawtooth Forest bird guide. Along waterways the most usual sightings are water ouzel (dipper), belted kingfisher, killdeer, spotted sandpiper, common merganser, and Mallard duck. Also present are the fish-eating osprey, especially near the Sawtooth Fish Hatchery and Redfish and Stanley lakes.

The common snipe (who covets fenceposts), marsh hawk, white-crowned sparrow, yellow warbler, red-winged blackbird, and the unmistakable, three-foot-tall greater sandhill crane can be found in meadows and willows. The Idaho state bird, the mountain bluebird, thrives in some locations. Look for them along the first few miles of Cabin Creek Road (between Pettit and Alturas Lake) or take trip 36, the lake-to-lake bike ride. Another colorful bird to watch for is the western tanager.

In campgrounds are the boisterous gray and white Clark's nutcracker, the Steller's jay (bluejay), magpie, and raven.

Birds of prey in addition to the osprey and marsh hawk include red-tailed hawks, common nighthawks, and golden eagles. Bald eagles are sometimes seen along the Salmon River and other waterways. The great horned owl serenades through mountain evenings. Hummingbirds are found at all altitudes and hikers may be startled to find themselves buzzed by fluorescent-colored hummers.

To some folks, a vacation *is* fishing. Central Idaho lakes, rivers, and streams provide it. Fishing pressure is heavy for rainbow trout in the Big Wood River and Salmon River along Highway 75. The Department of Fish and Game frequently restocks these waters with hatchery fish.

Hiking fishermen will find backcountry lakes and streams with good-sized (and often persnickety) trout, especially cutthroat and eastern brook trout, sometimes golden trout, grayling, and Dolly Varden. Tackle stores have all the where-to and how-to information.

Anadromous (ocean-going) fish—steelhead trout and chinook salmon—spawn in the Salmon River and its tributaries. There is presently no salmon fishing season in central Idaho, although there is a limited steelhead season.

THE WILDERNESS STATE

Idaho has more wild land—some 16 million acres—than any other state but Alaska, but only one-fourth of it is officially protected in the National Wilderness Preservation System.

Wilderness designation by Congress keeps public lands wild by prohibiting roading, logging, and all mechanized use (including bicycles). The law defines wilderness as "an area where earth and community life are untrammeled by man, where man himself is a visitor who does not remain." Hiking, camping, horseback riding, skiing, hunting, fishing, grazing, and mining (on valid claims) are all allowed. And the primary natural values—watershed, fish and wildlife, and open spaces—are protected as they are.

The natural and economic values of wilderness are steadily becoming recognized. Recreation is now Idaho's third largest industry and quickly becoming the second. Studies show that people come to Idaho for the "scenic beauty," "uncrowded atmosphere," and "to escape to the outdoors." Wilderness recreation is affordable and accessible. Families can vacation on public lands in or near wilderness areas with a minimum of cost or gear.

The Frank Church–River of No Return Wilderness (designated in 1980) is the largest in the lower 48 states—2.3 million acres, or as big as Yellowstone Park. This wilderness protects Idaho's most famous white-water river, the Middle Fork of the Salmon, and nearly its entire watershed. Frank Church's name was added to the wilderness in 1983, a month before his death. Church was the Idaho Senator who did more than any other person to bring it into being. He was also a key figure in enacting the Wilderness Act itself in 1964 and the Wild and Scenic Rivers bill in 1968.

The 217,000-acre Sawtooth Wilderness was designated when the SNRA was created in 1972 (again, thanks to Frank Church). Many of the hikes in this book explore trails, canyons, lakes, and historical places in or near this wilderness.

Trails. The paths of Sawtooth land are a heritage built by blisters, sore backs, and, for the most part, funds. Budgets for trail maintenance and reconstruction are slim; so are dollars for wilderness education, which helps prevent many of the impacts that trail crews must repair.

There's opportunity to volunteer for trail work. Groups such as the Idaho Conservation League (ICL) cooperate with local ranger districts to maintain trails and rehabilitate backcountry campsites. Volunteers work with a trained leader and rebuild or clean out waterbars that help curb trail erosion, recut the tread on sloughing sections, remove rocks from the path, trim overhanging branches and brush, improve stream crossings, eliminate unnecessary fire rings, and pick up litter.

Activities

If you're a new backcountry traveler or new to Sawtooth Country, plunge in—begin with short trips on well-maintained trails. Experience will bring confidence and conditioning.

FAMILIES AFIELD

Easy does it. Kids love the outdoors—or will if given the chance. Use the short hike and bike lists and the trip matrix (see Appendices) to find a trip within your limits. Car camping and day hiking are good places to start before committing to backpacking trips. Once competent, try abandoning motorization and pack in a mile or two, for a day or two.

Adults seize panoramas; little folks gaze toward camouflaged frogs. Expect frequent stops to examine glittery quartz, an ant housing development, a school of minnows, or dewdrops upon a spider web. Look for wildlife and flowers. Wise adults store up jokes, songs, and games to ward off whining and boredom. Bring plenty of tasty food, and stow away treats for a spirit-lifting surprise.

CAMPING

Pay Campgrounds. Run by the Forest Service or privately, these campgrounds include improvements such as tables, fireplace and cooking grills, drinking water, restrooms, trash pickup, and, at a few areas, electrical outlets. Reservations may be necessary at Redfish, Stanley, and Alturas lakes during busy summer weekends and may be made in advance with the Stanley Ranger Station or SNRA headquarters.

Free Sites. Countless unimproved, free camping sites that have been used for decades are scattered throughout Sawtooth Country's vast public lands. From May to October, scores of trailers, motor homes, pick-up campers, and tents dot the countryside, especially along the lower lakes, Salmon River, and Big Wood River.

Backcountry Campsites. For those who shun campgrounds and motors, a little effort will leave noise and development behind. Families can backpack just a short distance from their car and gain a mini-wilderness experience. For those willing to walk, camping choices are never ending.

HIKING

Day Hiking. The focus of this book is day hiking. Many trails are just minutes away from the communities of Stanley, Ketchum, and Sun Valley or nearby campgrounds. Day hiking takes less preparation than backpacking, is a lightweight means of travel to see miles of new country, and allows you to return to the comfort of an established camp, motel, or residence at night. For many Idahoans with limited time, the streamlined mode of day hiking is a way of life.

Backpacking. Nearly all the hikes can be extended into overnight trips. (Often when day trekking you'll wish you could stay longer!) Another possibility, combine two or more day hikes for a backpack trip. The book's lengthier trips can be backpacked over a leisurely three-day weekend. Destinations interesting and suitable for youngsters are plentiful in Sawtooth Country. Determine beforehand whether camping is limited or fires restricted. For information on other guidebooks that emphasize backpack trips, see Further Reading in the appendices or contact local ranger districts.

Scrambling. This is the nickname given to off-trail, upward wanders that require more energy and attention than casual walking on designated paths. Few of this book's trips require scrambling unless you so choose. The notable exceptions: Washington Peak and Hyndman Peak. Both are considered "walk-ups"—meaning that technical climbing equipment is not required and you can literally walk (or scramble) to the top. At least a dozen other trips make reference to scrambling opportunities.

Safety. The trip descriptions will help you make choices about what outing is suitable for your needs and often suggest the best month and weather conditions to go. From May through mid-July, stream crossings are often an important factor in choosing destinations. The text will mention these. Basic information for safely enjoying hiking or scrambling is given under PRECAUTIONS later in this introduction. Learn more by reading books focusing on outdoor skills.

MOUNTAIN BIKING

If you're a newcomer to fat-tired biking and the recreational hubs of Stanley, Ketchum, and Sun Valley, you'll notice the abundance of mountain bikes—on the streets and on rooftop car carriers.

Unlike motorbikes, bicycles move quietly through the hills, powered solely by muscle. On trails musclebikes can be lifted over obstacles such as logs and boulders and portaged through streams. Backroads come to be savored when they are pedaled rather than driven. Often, mountain biking is hard work and more strenuous than hiking. But for every grind uphill there's a downhill waiting.

When you ride out to the hills, be aware that not everyone is enthusiastic about bicyclists flooding backcountry trails. Traditional users—hikers, horsemen, stockmen, fishermen, and hunters (even those who also own mountain bikes)—may be startled and resent the careening intrusion of bicycles. Slow down and be courteous. This book will steer you away from trails that receive heavy hiker and horse use. Foot travelers and horsemen have long had their niche on public lands. For bicyclists, that niche is still to be carved.

It is The Mountaineers' policy that bike trips be outside of designated or proposed wilderness. *Adventures in Idaho's Sawtooth Country* follows this stipulation and heartily endorses it. Many areas in the Boulder–White Clouds, Smoky Mountains, and Pioneers are awaiting Congressionally designated wilderness status. This book will help you discover the abundant roads and trails outside of these areas.

Bike Rentals and Service. There are numerous bike shops in Ketchum and

Sun Valley that sell, rent, and service bicycles—some year-round. Bike rentals are also available in Stanley and at various resorts in the Sawtooth Valley. Check with local Chamber of Commerce offices or local phone directories for bicycle outlets.

Tykes and Bikes. Family bike rides require more careful planning than family hikes. Longer distances are involved and so are mechanical machines that may break down. Use this book's list of short bike rides to match kids to terrain. If you're unsure about a route, scout it first. Uphills, headwinds, and soft or rocky road surfaces may overwhelm a youngster's strength or mental perseverance. Consider how difficult the return portion of a ride will be. Be creative—use a vehicle on long uphill sections and let the kids ride the flats or downhills. The entire family should wear helmets. Warn youngsters about the hazards of loose sand or gravel as well as traffic. Have a plan for dealing with flat tires and repairs. On longer trips, a child needs a properly fit, reasonably lightweight mountain bike.

Safety and Etiquette. Mountain biking requires special attention to safety and etiquette.

- Wear a helmet. Especially on rough trails.
- Keep groups small. Bikers or any users traveling in a large pack diminishes the backcountry experience for themselves and others.
- Carry a first aid kit and the other Ten Essentials (more on that later). Painful abrasions or cuts when extremities are scraped against rocks, branches, or sharp pedals will happen.
- Carry a repair kit (a biker's Eleventh Essential). Learn to fix flat tires and problems with chains, cables, and derailleurs. Carry a spare tube on long trips. Bike shops often offer free maintenance clinics.
- Carry water. Follow all warnings in this introduction regarding *Giardia.*
- Pack a windbreaker, preferably with a hood, for chilly headwinds. Also helpful are gloves, long-sleeved shirt, and windpants. Count on afternoon winds.
- A bicycle eats up the miles until trouble strikes. A breakdown may necessitate a long walk out or an overnight bivouack. All group members on long trips to remote areas should understand the possible hazards and be prepared, gear-wise and attitude-wise.
- Watch for horses and hikers. The silence of bicycles can be downright dangerous to horseback riders and pack strings. Use extra caution on narrow, curvy trails. Dismount your bike and move downhill, off the trail. Speak, so the animal recognizes you as human.
- Avoid riding on wet trails or meadows. Tires leave ruts which act as water channels and accelerate erosion. Wheel furrows can drain a wet area, causing vegetation to dry up. Carry your bike rather than ride through bogs or springs.
- Rock or log waterbars are installed on trails to direct water and prevent erosion. Respect these resource protectors—they take 2 hours or more to properly build. Either ride directly over the top of

a waterbar or dismount. Avoid riding around the ends—this causes a channel to develop, which allows water to wash down the trail. Most waterbars in Sawtooth Country were not made for wheels, but for legs that can step over them.

- Skidding or locking up wheels—a problem on steep grades—leads to trail deterioration. So does skidding around switchbacks. Recognize the need to sometimes walk or shoulder your bike. Avoid adopting the macho attitude that discourages this caution and causes resource damage as a result. Remember—abuse it, you'll lose it.
- When riding downhill, lower the bike seat so your feet can quickly touch the ground and perhaps prevent a fall. Most mountain bikes come equipped with a quick-release seat lever.
- Anticipate hills and shift beforehand, without pressure on the pedals.
- Deflate tires slightly on rocky surfaces to lessen the jolting ride, re-inflate on smoother surfaces. Check tires before every ride and maintain proper pressure. Watch for sharp rocks or branches that can poke a tire's sidewall and quickly cause a flat.
- Wash your bike after riding in mud or sand; re-oil chain and other parts.

Maps

The maps in this book should be supplemented with the appropriate Forest Service (Sawtooth or Challis Forest) and USGS (United States Geological Survey) topographical map indicated under each trip. Forest Service maps are sold at ranger stations. They provide a broad overview and will be adequate for most bike trips and hikes on well-defined trails.

A USGS topo map is more detailed and has contour lines, which allows you to anticipate the type of terrain ahead—the closer together the contour lines, the steeper the slope. Most of the topo maps for this area are 7¹/₂-minute series with a scale of 1:24,000 (1 inch equals 2,000 feet). A USGS map and a compass are strongly recommended for most hikes in new surroundings and for off-trail exploring. When using a USGS map, note the year it was published. Maps for areas in this book are usually 15 to 20 years old. Many trails have been rerouted or in some cases are no longer maintained and may be difficult to find. These discrepancies will be noted in the trip descriptions. Also, older USGS maps will not show new mining or logging roads. Again, the text will inform you of this. USGS maps are sold by local outdoor stores and ranger stations.

For hiking in the Sawtooth Wilderness, Earthwalk Press has published a 1:48,000 topo map (1 inch equals about 1.2 miles) that covers the entire wilderness. It's sold by ranger stations and local outdoor stores. Although it is an excellent map, USGS maps are still the best choice for off-trail route finding.

Because of the wide vistas and open country in much of Sawtooth Country, many summer hikers seldom use a compass and rely solely on topo maps. Nevertheless, bring a compass along and practice using it to find off-trail lakes or to identify distant peaks. Familiarize yourself with it so you can use it should you get lost. If you rarely use a compass, keep directions with it in your pack.

Deciding What to Take

THE TEN ESSENTIALS

Gather these into your backpack as naturally as you tie your boot laces. Go prepared. When adventure calls, a 2-hour hike can stretch to nightfall. Some items may be carried, unused, on 100 day trips—but when needed, they're priceless.

1. Extra clothing
2. Extra food and water
3. Map
4. Compass
5. Flashlight, extra batteries, bulb
6. Knife
7. Matches (in waterproof container) or lighter
8. Firestarter
9. First aid kit including blister kit and insect repellent
10. Sunglasses and sunscreen

BOOTS AND BLISTERS

Lightweight hiking boots of leather or leather and nylon blend are used by Sawtooth hikers. Sturdy running shoes will suffice, but they don't protect from foot-bruising rocky trails. Soles need good traction for safety on steep grades and wet ground, rocks, or logs.

Wear socks made for hiking—a thin undersock and a thicker outer sock of wool or polypro-wool blend will cushion the foot and help prevent blisters (eliminate the inner sock if boot feels too snug).

Boots (and feet) should be broken in before long hikes or multiday trips. Many hikers who know their feet are not trail-toughened bring along tennis shoes. Cushioned insoles are excellent shock absorbers and foot protectors; make sure they fit precisely within the boot.

Carry a blister first-aid packet. Experiment with various shapes and sizes of donuts to take pressure away from hot spots or blisters. Blister remedies are available in drug stores and include: adhesive knit, moleskin, waterproof tape, and small, folding scissors. Tend to a foot's hot spot immediately, before a blister develops. Blisters are serious business. Left unattended they can become infected and incapacitating.

BACKPACKING GEAR

If you use this guidebook for backpacking trips, there are a few pointers for overnighting in the Sawtooth backcountry. A tent is essential to provide shelter from frequent thunderstorms and will also provide warmth on chilly nights —summer frost is common at higher elevations. A tent also provides relief from insects.

Sleeping bags made of a nylon outer material and filled with synthetic insulation are lightweight and dry quickly if wet. Avoid canvas bags with flannel linings; they are heavy to carry and absorb moisture.

For cooking bring a lightweight backpacking stove and follow directions for its use precisely (practice at home first). A stove is a quick and efficient way to boil water and prepare food, and using one spares the scarce wood in alpine areas. Carry your stove and fuel canister in a separate pack pocket from clothing or food.

Backpacking equipment can be rented in Ketchum and Stanley from outdoor stores. Check local phone directories or the Chamber of Commerce office for rental sources. It's best to call well in advance to reserve gear. Whether buying or renting a backpack, have it custom-fit by an experienced salesperson.

BE WEATHERPROOF

The following list will help you be weatherproof for summer trips in this book. For short outings, only a sweater and windbreaker may be needed. However, most of these items are standard gear for hikers who've been nibbled by black flies in June, drenched by July rain, and snowed on in August. As you broaden your backcountry experience, invest in clothing that's an asset wet or dry. Idaho backpacking stores brim with choices.

- Windbreaker with hood
- Hiking shorts (loose, fast drying)
- Cotton T-shirt
- Sun hat
- Sweater or shirt (wool or synthetic)
- Rain gear, jacket and pants
- Polypro long-sleeve shirt
- Polypro long johns
- Long pants (loose, fast drying)
- Wool or polypro gloves or mitts (or both)
- Overmitts (nylon or waterproof breathable synthetic)
- Storm hat (wool or polypro)
- Nylon rain poncho (can be worn or used as emergency shelter)

Polypro is short for polypropylene, a synthetic material used in shirts and underwear that is amazingly warm for its weight. It wicks moisture away from the skin, absorbs little water, and dries quickly. Hikers also use "polypro" generically, referring to synthetic garments, whatever the fabric content, as polypro. Synthetic pile is thicker and warmer than polypro but has similar characteristics. Follow care directions carefully, especially avoiding hot dryers.

HIGH-ALTITUDE SUN

Sun burns quickly in the clear, thin mountain air. A hat, sunglasses, sunscreen, and lipcream are essential protection. Mountain sun may cause fair-skinned persons to suffer painful cold sores about the lips unless a sunblock lipcream is used repeatedly during and after sun exposure.

INSECTS

Insect repellent is one of the Ten Essentials, but even "bug juice" doesn't always deter insects. Wind and cold are their worst foes. Black flies may torment hikers at all elevations. Hats and thick, bite-resistant, long-sleeved shirts and pants will stave them off. At certain times mosquitoes and flies can be so thick that abandoning the trip and going elsewhere is prudent.

Ticks are unpleasant little insects found at lower elevations, especially in sagebrush. Tick season starts in the spring and continues into the fall until a hard freeze. Frequent inspections will keep ticks from adhering too deeply in your skin. Check pets, too. First aid books recommend removing ticks with tweezers or covering a tick with oil so it will disengage itself within half an hour. Cleanse the area with soap and water. Most ticks are just an annoyance, but they can transmit serious illnesses: Rocky Mountain spotted fever, tick paralysis, and Lyme disease. If a red rash, fever, aches, weakness, or lethargy occurs, get medical help.

Outdoor Etiquette

Gone are the mountain-man days when log lean-tos, fir-bough beds, and roaring fires were part of camping. The ethic of **low-impact, no-trace** camping needs to be practiced by all recreationists—from motor-home dwellers to horsemen, from backpackers to river runners. There are just too many of us to do otherwise. The information here applies to the mountain environment. Low-impact techniques may differ along rivers and coasts and in desert lands. The book *Soft Paths*, listed in Further Reading, has more information.

CHOOSING A CAMPSITE

At lakes and other popular areas, it's obvious where others have camped before. Use the same sites to avoid tramping additional ground (though some over-used places may be posted No Camping). Pitch tents on sand, dirt, or a forest floor of dried pine needles where you won't damage fragile alpine plants. If you use a meadow or grassy area, move your tent daily. Leave a site cleaner than you found it, and sweep disturbed soil with a dead branch or stick to erase tent lines.

CAMPFIRES

In some areas campfires may be restricted due to scarce wood or fire danger. Be aware of both.

When the wind blows be extra careful. Sparks can ignite branches or nearby grass or scorch tents. Always attend your fire or put it out—dead out. Use water and dirt and stir the embers. Carelessness causes forest fires.

When car camping, pay campgrounds may furnish firewood to protect nearby trees from being cut or limbs broken off to be burned. You also can gather deadfall by hand along back roads.

When backpacking use a stove; it's efficient for cooking and spares wood. Some alpine lakes prohibit campfires. Respect this closure since it's done to protect what few trees grow at high elevations.

Wherever you are, please be protective of Sawtooth Country's magnificent, bleached hulks of long-dead, but still standing, whitebark pines. A campfire lasts only a few minutes, but a rotting log will nourish the high country indefinitely.

LITTER

Thoughtful preplanning of a trip's food supply will help decrease what is carried in full and carried out empty. Learn what is biodegradable and what isn't. Tossing bread crusts or apple cores into the bushes may provide a snack for pine squirrels (or bears), but orange and banana peels must be carried out— both take months to decompose.

If you burn peelings or foil in a campfire, sift through the ashes and tote home any non-biodegradable substance. If you smoke, accept the responsibility to pack out the cigarette butts. The rule is simple—pack out what you packed in.

PERSONAL HYGIENE

A large part of the wilderness ethic is proper disposal of waste and protection of backcountry water quality. Just when we've been trained to think like a cat and bury human waste, studies have shown buried feces decompose slowly, while sun and air greatly speed up decomposition. With this in mind, outdoorsmen should adjust their sanitation rituals depending on location.

Near popular trails or lakes use the cat-hole technique at least 100 feet from any water source: dig several inches deep into soil, mix the feces with dirt, cover with more dirt and humus, and disguise the top layer so that no trace of disturbance remains. In certain areas—200 feet away from water sources and well away from any trail and possible discovery by other humans—feces can be mixed with soil and left on the surface to decompose.

Adopt the habit of using natural toilet paper—leaves, grass, moss, bark, smooth rocks, snow. Toilet paper left in a cat-hole may be dug up by an animal. Double-bag toilet tissue to either burn in a campfire or carry out. The same goes for tampons and sanitary napkins. If there's no danger of igniting nearby grass or dry conifer needles, toilet paper can be burned with a match. However, this practice has started more than one forest or range fire, so be cautious. Pet feces need to be disposed of the same way as human waste.

CLEANING UP

Help avoid polluting water and harming aquatic life by avoiding the use of soap or shampoo, biodegradable or otherwise, in streams, hot springs, rivers, or lakes. For cleaning dishes (or yourself) haul water for rinsing and washing to a gravelly or rocky area away from lakes and streams. Leftover food should be packed out or widely scattered far from camp. Buried leftovers will be dug up by animals. Consider the ease of cleanup when planning backcountry meals.

DOGS

So far, pets are not restricted in Sawtooth Country. However, with increasing use in all backcountry areas, dog owners are being asked to follow the same rules for disposing of pet feces as their own. This helps protect water quality and asthetics and makes canines and their masters more agreeable to other users.

Leash a sedentary pet to save its energy and prevent sore paws. Also, control a dog if it chases wildlife. When hiking or biking past one of the many bands of sheep that graze throughout the summer and fall in the Sawtooth Forest, you'll often encounter guard dogs. They can be aggressive toward other animals. Keep your pet by your side and away from the flock.

Precautions

AM I LOST?

Anyone who has been "turned around" in the woods knows the enveloping, chilling feeling. Always carry the Ten Essentials and learn the use of map and compass. Everyone in a group should familiarize themselves with the route and destination. Frequently glance back at where you've been for landmarks. Know when darkness falls and plan accordingly.

The open vistas of central Idaho mountain ranges lessen the likelihood of becoming totally lost. Yet, an active search-and-rescue network in this area rescues several persons every year. When hopeless confusion blurs any sense of which way to go, accept being lost.

- Sit down, remain calm, promise yourself not to panic
- Keep all members of a group together
- Stay in one place (well sheltered), mark the spot
- Plan ahead for nightfall
- Build a fire in a safe location where flames won't spread
- Make yourself noticeable to searchers
- If you have a whistle, use it to blow three short blasts—the universal distress signal

FOR KIDS: "HUG-A-TREE"

Parents should review the following procedures with their children in the event a child becomes separated from the hiking group.

- Wear a whistle on picnics, hikes, and camping trips. It takes less energy to use and carries farther than a voice.

- Carry a trash bag in your daypack to be used as an emergency shelter. Make a hole for the face.
- Wear bright clothes (red, orange, yellow).
- Lost? Hug a tree. Stay by it. Talk to it. Name it. Save your energy.
- Find shelter from the wind by your tree.
- Know that many volunteers are searching.
- Being lost is okay. No one will be mad.
- Make yourself big. If possible, find your friendly tree near a meadow or clearing, where your bright colored clothes or pack will be more likely to catch attention. Make crosses or an SOS out of branches, bushes, or rocks.
- No animals will hurt you although you may hear their footsteps and noises. This is their home. Don't be afraid.
- Find a pastime—whittling, singing, building a village of twigs and stones.

A brochure called *Hug a Tree and Survive* is available from Blaine County Search & Rescue, Box 583, Hailey, ID 83333.

GOING SOLO

Most guidebooks tell you not to hike or bike alone. This one won't do that. Half of this book's trips were done solo. However, three is an ideal number in a trekking party. If someone is hurt, one member goes for help, and one stays with the injured. Novice hikers are wise to use well-marked trails.

When traveling alone, know your limits and save heroics for an accompanied trek. Leave word of your destination and expected time of return with a friend or at a ranger station (be sure to check in on your return), or jot a note for the kitchen table. A note can also be left in your car at the trailhead. All these precautions may seem like a bother. But no one ever *expects* to be lost. Or injured.

WATER

A hiker on a warm, day-long trek may require 2 quarts or more of water. On strenuous trips it's easy to drink a gallon. Water filters are becoming standard equipment because all open water must be assumed to harbor the *Giardia* parasite—even chilled, clear, rushing streams. Drinking water infected with the *Giardia* parasite can cause giardiasis, also called beaver fever, and bring on fatigue, diarrhea, stomach cramps, vomiting, and general misery. Symptoms usually occur in 8 to 14 days but may appear as early as 4 days or as late as 6 weeks after drinking contaminated water.

Giardia is spread through human and animal feces which then contaminate water. Since the *Giardia* parasite tolerates extreme cold, but not heat, the best protection is to boil water. Five to 10 minutes at a rolling boil is the widely used norm in the high-altitude Sawtooth Country. (The greater the fear, the longer the boil.) Or you may use a filter designed to screen out *Giardia* cysts.

All water that touches lips, including that for brushing teeth, should be filtered or boiled. Avoid rinsing dishes or water bottles in streams or lakes or swallowing water when washing or swimming. Clean your hands before handling food and after going to the toilet. Be especially suspicious of open water after rain or near campsites, beaver ponds, and grazing areas. Try to obtain drinking water from the source of springs or side streams. Help curb the spread of *Giardia* by burying human or dog feces at least 100 feet away from waterways.

LIGHTNING

Beginning in May and continuing through summer, rotund cotton pillars churn skyward—evidence of developing thunderstorms. Since thundershowers usually occur in the afternoon, an early start may see you off high ridges or mountain passes before lightning, rain, hail, and gusty winds move in. But forecasting is a guess. One storm can follow another, and another.

Lightning will hit ahead of storm clouds, before rain begins. Heed warning signs. The sound of thunder travels 5 seconds per mile. A flash of lightning followed by thunder 15 seconds later indicates a strike just 3 miles away. Take cover.

- Make yourself small; don't be the tallest object on a ridge, slope, meadow, or lakeshore.
- Move away from natural lightning rods and good electrical conductors: lone trees, small groups of tall trees, rock outcroppings, small buildings in open spaces, metal, moist areas, streams and lakes. A direct strike is not necessary to cause severe injury.
- Seek shelter in dense woods, thick clumps of trees or brush, swales, gullies, or ditches (but not ones with water).
- If caught in the open, squat down (don't sit) with feet close together, hands on knees and keep head bowed. This stance minimizes your height and limits contact points with the ground.
- A close strike is imminent when the odor of ozone appears, skin tingles, or hair stands on end. Immediately take the squat position.
- Give CPR immediately to a person struck by lightning.

Be aware of other hazards accompanying thunderstorms: strong winds can blow down shallow-rooted firs and pines; a downpour of rain and hail can cause floodwaters to rush down creeks and dry washes.

HYPOTHERMIA

Storms occur in the mountains. Snow may fall in every month in Idaho's mountains. Afternoon thunderstorms may be followed by fog and drizzle, which may linger through the night.

As you explore deeper and higher into the backcountry (and some all-day trips in this book take you there) be prepared to take shelter before becoming soaked and shivering. Learn to recognize the signs of hypothermia—when the body's internal temperature is lowered to a point where mental and physical impairment occurs. If not reversed, hypothermia can cause death.

Being wet, chilled, exposed to the wind, and overexerted are causes of hypothermia. The symptoms are shivering, cold skin, vague movements, fumbling and stumbling, and incoherent speech. Treatment consists of preventing additional heat loss (get out of wind, rain, or snow); removing wet clothing and rewarming with dry clothes, a sleeping bag, or another person's body warmth; giving warm drinks only if conscious (but not alcohol); and building a fire.

To prevent hypothermia, carry the Ten Essentials and bivouac or camp early—before you're soaked and freezing. Avoid overexertion. Monitor your party members for hypothermia symptoms. Thin individuals can take less cold than their heavier companions. Keep dry. Carry an emergency shelter and know how to quickly use it. Remember that blue jeans, cotton, and down-filled garments are worthless when wet.

SCRAMBLING

The line distinguishing scramblers from climbers is vague, but generally scramblers maneuver upwards on "safe," nontechnical routes, where ropes are not needed, and a fall, if one occurs, means a bruise or abrasion, not a serious injury. Even casual hikers sometimes become scramblers when trails are steep, washed out, or snow covered.

Tips for scramblers:

- Don't climb unprotected (i.e., without a rope) any distance greater than you'd want to fall. Select routes and objectives on that premise.
- When climbing, have three secure points (two hands, one foot or two feet, one hand) before reaching for the fourth. Test new footholds or handholds for stability.
- Keep body weight centered over the feet—don't hug the rock.
- Move smoothly. In tight spots, stay calm, avoid rushing, talk to yourself, keep your humor.
- Experienced scramblers can reassure nervous companions by staying close, offering advice, and relieving the tension with a few jokes.
- On rocky slopes, move one person at a time to avoid rolling debris on a companion below. Once the person lowest in the group has descended a section, that person should move aside, out of the path of possible rockfall.
- Be careful of snow cornices—the overhanging mass of snow or ice caused by wind on mountain ridges. By summer most have melted past the point of breaking away but use caution when crossing or traveling below. Another hazard to avoid is thawing ice or snow near lakeshores or over streams; it may be hollow underneath and break with your weight.
- Respect fears of party members. Take them seriously. Novice scramblers can gain confidence through practice. A little challenge is exhilarating, too much is terrorizing. Turn back.
- Bring along a security rope. Intended as a security line and not a full-on climbing rope, a 60-foot length of $5/16$-inch nylon rope can be tied around a hiker's waist so a companion can belay him safely over the problem.

GLISSADING

Long, gravel-strewn slopes of scree as well as snowfields can provide a fast, rollicking glissade after a tedious climb to a ridgeline or summit. Glissading is like skiing without skis as you slide downward on your boot soles. Amusing as glissading can be, it's also potentially dangerous. Accidents happen because unwary hikers venture onto frozen slopes for a quick descent and zoom their way into crevasses or boulder fields or over cliffs. When in doubt, don't. Leave the shortcut to trained, ice-ax–equipped mountaineers.

Parts of Sawtooth Country, especially in the Pioneers, White Clouds, and Boulders, have long chutes of scree. Before you start down, make certain the entire line of descent is visible, then go one person at a time down the chute. Scree skiing is very hard on footwear.

CROSSING WATER

Early-season hikers may encounter high, snowmelt-fed streams. Later in the summer, however, such streams may be easily forded. Wading barefoot is only for narrow, shallow creeks. Otherwise shoes are key to maintaining balance on hard, slippery stones. If wading or log-walking is your nemesis, check out trail conditions with local ranger stations before departing and perhaps go elsewhere.

- Wade in wider parts of the creek where the water is shallower.
- Avoid wading knee deep. Currents can sweep you off your feet.
- Use a walking stick or pole for balance.
- Stronger, more experienced woodsmen can help those who are not.
- If footing is lost, go with the current and work your way to shore.
- Crossing logs above frothing water calls for sure footing and steady nerves. Practice beforehand at any convenient log along the trail. Some logs can be straddled, as in riding a horse, and crossed inch by inch.
- Retreat if necessary.

MINE TUNNELS AND SHAFTS

Old mine tunnels and shafts are numerous throughout the mountain ranges in this book. Exploring them is not recommended. Possible cave-ins, vertical shafts that may be covered by pools of water or debris, and bad air (or lack of oxygen) are hazards. When hiking or camping with children, be extra careful of these sites, and scout your surroundings before letting kids go unsupervised. Avoid drinking water from sources below tailing piles.

BEARS

Sawtooth Country is black bear country. Black bears are not generally aggressive or dangerous, though sows with cubs need the utmost respect.

Some bears wander into campgrounds, attracted by dumpsters. Take all precautions to discourage bear visits. NEVER give handouts. A bear used to receiving food from humans will become a "problem" bear. Feeding them is signing their death warrant. Don't do it. Help bears avoid trouble.

- Keep a clean camp. Store food in a closed vehicle or suspended on a branch, out of bear reach (remember cubs can climb). Never store food in a tent. Treat garbage the same as food. Never bury or scatter it around camp.
- Avoid using odorous foods. Don't sleep in clothes you cook in.
- On backcountry trips, burn fish entrails in a hot campfire or punc-

ture air sacks on the viscera and toss far into a lake or fast-moving stream.

- Black bears are shy and will avoid humans. Don't surprise them. Talk, sing, whistle, travel in groups, and hike in daylight hours.
- Learn bear sign: overturned rocks or logs, clawed-up ant piles or decaying stumps, human-like excrement but with remnants of seeds, pine nuts, roots, or undigested dumpster meals.
- Leash your dog—it may bring a bear back to you.
- If a cub is encountered, leave the area immediately.
- When encountering a bear, talk. They have good ears but bad eyes. Your voice will let them identify you and possibly scare them off.
- Bears may stand up on their hind legs for a better look or smell; don't be alarmed.
- Stand still, do not run. If the bear seems nonaggressive, back away.
- If a charge appears imminent (unlikely), look for a tree to climb. As you're heading toward it, drop a pack, a jacket, something to distract the bear.
- Should the worst happen, wrap yourself in a ball and play dead.

How to Use This Book

ORGANIZATION

The hiking and mountain biking trips in this book are separated into geographic areas, starting in the northern part of Sawtooth Country with Stanley and the Salmon River Mountains. The Sawtooth Mountains and the White Cloud Mountains in the central part of the region come next. Trips in the Ketchum and Sun Valley area feature outings in the Smoky Mountains, Boulder Mountains, and the west side of the Pioneer Mountains.

Each trip description contains a block summarizing important information about each hike or bike ride (see below). Additional alternative trips, side trips, and turnaround points are included with many of the trips.

CHOOSING A TRIP

The table of contents will help you choose a trip for the area you want to visit. Consult the trip matrix (see Appendices) for a quick overview of each trip's features, including its difficulty rating, the type of access road, whether car camping or backpacking is available along the route, and other features, such as historical sights or scenic drives. Use the lists of short hikes and easy bike rides (see Appendices) for a quick summary of briefer trips, many of which are suitable for families with young children or seniors. See individual trip descriptions and information blocks for complete details on these trips.

INFORMATION BLOCKS

This summary of information helps you assess and choose a trip that will best suit your interests, time, and skill level. It gives the main activity described in the text (hiking or biking) as well as other opportunities available on the trip. It gives the total mileage and whether the trip is one-way, and thus requiring a car shuttle; a round trip; or a loop.

Each trip also is rated for its difficulty. The ratings—easy, moderate, strenuous, and difficult—are arbitrary and target the average hiker or biker in good physical condition. Trail conditions or weather may affect these ratings.

An easy rating indicates that a trail or road is fairly short in length, easy to follow, and has minimal change in elevation. A moderate rating covers a broad scope, and some "moderate" trips may be more difficult than others. Read the trip description for details. A strenuous rating usually means the trip is on a designated trail, but is arduous because of elevation gain or long distance. A trip is rated difficult if it contains any one of the following: route finding off the trail, a faded or hard-to-follow path, an unmaintained or seldom-maintained trail, a stream crossing, or scrambling.

The trip's highest elevation point as well as the elevation gain, measured from the beginning of the trip to the trip's high point, are listed.

Bike trips contain information on the different road surfaces a rider can expect to encounter, be it pavement, gravel, cobbles, sand, or dirt.

All trips indicate the months when a road or trail is free of snow. In some cases, hikers and bikers also need to be aware of stream crossings. Late spring and early summer snowmelt can make stream crossings difficult. Check at local ranger stations or hiking and biking shops about conditions.

In addition to the maps in the book, you should also bring along a Sawtooth or Challis National Forest map and/or a USGS topographical map as indicated in the information block. Purchase forest maps, Sawtooth National Recreation Area (SNRA) maps, and Sawtooth Wilderness maps at the local ranger station. USGS maps, or topos, are recommended for hiking trips with a moderate or greater rating. Purchase these at ranger stations or local outdoor stores. When a trip covers more than one topo map, the maps are listed in order of importance. A Forest Service map will suffice for most trips, and the text will tell you when a topo map is needed.

A Note About Safety

Safety is an important concern in all outdoor activities. No guidebook can alert you to every hazard or anticipate the limitations of every reader. Therefore, the descriptions of roads, trails, routes, and natural features in this book are not representations that a particular place or excursion will be safe for your party. When you follow any of the routes described in this book, you assume responsibility for your own safety. Under normal conditions, such excursions require the usual attention to traffic, road and trail conditions, weather, terrain, the capabilities of your party, and other factors. Keeping informed on current conditions and exercising common sense are the keys to a safe, enjoyable outing.

The Mountaineers

Stanley and
Salmon River Mountains

1 ROOKIE POINT

Best for: hiking
2 miles round trip
Moderate
Elevation gain: 497 feet
High point: 7,297 feet
Hikable: June through October
Maps: USGS Custer, Sunbeam

A short, pleasant hike on an unmaintained trail leads to Rookie Point over-looking Bonanza and the Yankee Fork River valley. Rookie Point was a mock lookout, used for training new fire spotters. Now all that remains of the old building are fragments of boards and old glass.

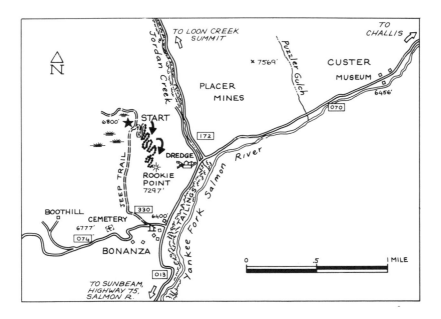

Storm over Marsh Creek meadowlands along Cape Horn Road

Dredge tailings in Yankee Fork River as seen from Rookie Point

From Stanley, go downriver on Highway 75 for 13 miles to Sunbeam Dam. Turn left up the Yankee Fork and go 3 miles on narrow, paved road 013, which becomes gravel when dredge tailings begin. For the next 4.5 miles to Bonanza, follow the rippled mounds of river rock—dredging's legacy. Turn left on road 074. In 0.2 mile, pass the Yankee Fork Guard Station and take dirt road 330 going right. Follow it 1 mile to a meadow and park (high clearance is needed for the last 0.5 mile). Rookie Point is on the timber-covered mountainside to the east above you.

Walk along the right side of the meadow, and start up a jeep road that curves to the right and dead-ends in 50 yards, where the trail to Rookie Point begins. The mile-long path zigzags up through the woods and is crisscrossed with elk trails. Skirt deadfall and with persistence you'll reach a saddle. Look northward through the firs for glimpses of colorful Greylock Mountain and Jordan Creek canyon. Climb south on a fading and increasingly rocky path to Rookie Point, where charred wood marks the old training site.

The mountain east, above the Yankee Fork valley, is Bonanza Peak. To the southwest is a less attractive scene—the wide swath of the 1985 East Basin Creek forest fire. Also visible is the dredged Yankee Fork River and modern mining activities at Preacher's Cove. On the descent, stay on the switchback packtrail, avoiding misleading game paths.

2 CUSTER MOTORWAY

Best for: mountain biking
Opportunities for: scenic drive, hiking
35.5 miles one way
Moderate to difficult
Elevation gain: 2,400 feet
High point: 8,800 feet
Riding surface: gravel, dirt, rock
Ridable: mid-June through October
Maps: USGS Custer, Elevenmile Creek, Bayhorse Lake

Turnaround at Eightmile Creek and McFadden Mine Road

14.8 miles and 22 miles round trip
Moderate
Elevation gain: 440 feet and 920 feet

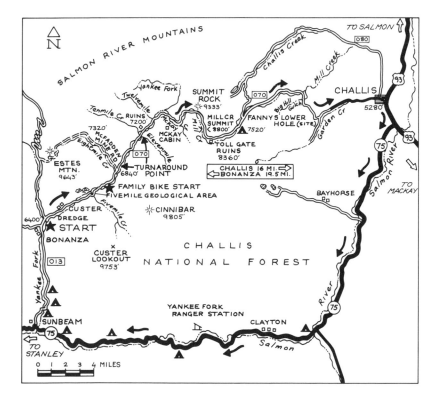

Turnaround at Elevenmile Station
22.8 miles round trip
Moderate
Elevation gain: 800 feet

The Custer Motorway began in 1879 as a toll road through the Salmon River Mountains from Challis to Bonanza City. Some sections are steep and rocky. Snow may linger until late June, so check with the Yankee Fork Ranger District about road conditions.

The description and mileage begin at Bonanza near the Yankee Fork of the Salmon River (see trip 1 for access). You may prefer to ride from Custer, avoiding 2 miles of dusty traffic and saving 4 miles on the round-trip distances listed for the turnaround points (families see alternative below). Along the motorway you'll go by eight streams named for their approximate distance from old Bonanza City, beginning with Fivemile Creek and ending with Twelvemile Creek. Expect ore trucks until 4th of July Creek, 2 miles beyond the Custer Museum.

While the motorway's 35-mile distance can be hiked using vehicle support, most cyclists choose round-trip rides from Bonanza or Custer. Pedaling the entire way to Challis is strenuous—you climb steadily until Mill Creek Summit (8,800 feet) and then face another hard pull over Big Hill Gulch near Challis.

After leaving Bonanza, ride past the dredge at 0.4 mile and reach Custer at 2 miles. At 4 miles, near Custer Campground No. 1, the road climbs steeply for 0.4 mile (the hardest pedal in the next 8 miles). A sign marks the Fivemile Geological Area, a jumble of rocks created by an ancient landfall that once dammed the canyon. (Trees largely block the view and the road is too narrow for safe vehicle parking.) Past the geological sign, a quick descent leads to Fivemile Creek—a good departure point for families, as the next 2.7 miles to Eightmile Creek wind nearly level through forest, along the sparkling Yankee Fork River.

Eightmile Creek (actually 7.4 miles from Bonanza) offers picnicking with views up Eightmile canyon. Bikers can turn around here and coast home. Or take a scenic side trip along Eightmile Creek on the primitive McFadden Mine road for about 3.6 miles. Along this mostly dirt track you'll be treated to washouts, stream crossings, and mud. Past the 3.6-mile mark, the McFadden Mine road eventually becomes difficult as it climbs to over 9,000 feet on Estes Mountain and then descends to Jordan Creek.

The road becomes rockier and steeper to 11.4 miles and the tumble-down Elevenmile Way Station where stages and freight wagons changed teams. Now the road climbs in earnest, leaving the Yankee Fork and turning right to reach a crossing of McKay Creek at 14 miles (called Twelvemile Crossing in the old days). In a meadow at 14.8 miles is McKay Cabin, another way station. Sum-

Eroded cliffs above the Yankee Fork River

mit Rock, landmark to wayfarers, is east. Leaving the willowed meadowlands, the cobbled road turns northeast up a gullied canyon, a tangle of lodgepole and mossy springs. At 18.6 miles is Mill Creek Summit. Then the road plunges downward. At 19.4 miles, reach Toll Gate and the ruins of three cabins. The second change of teams was done here. The motorway is now a widened, improved road as it drops to Mill Creek Campground at 21.7 miles.

From Fanny's Lower Hole, 22.7 miles, the road descends Mill Creek canyon for 5 miles, climbs a long 1.5 miles over Big Hill Gulch, and tops out in sagebrush at 29.3 miles. Below stretches Garden Creek. At 31 miles the road becomes paved and at 35.5 miles reaches Challis, a ranching and mining community in the beautiful Round Valley. It's 58 miles back to Stanley via Highway 75 along the Salmon River.

Alternative Ride: Fivemile Creek to Eightmile Creek
     5.4 miles round trip
     Easy, nearly level

Most of the motorway is too difficult for young riders, but a family outing could include a visit to Custer, followed by a drive to Fivemile Creek. Bike and explore the 2.7 miles to Eightmile Creek and have a picnic before returning to your car.

CHALLIS NATIONAL FOREST

3 BAYHORSE, BAYHORSE LAKES

     Best for: hiking
     Opportunities for: biking, scenic drive
     1.6 miles to 2 miles round trip
     Easy to moderate
     Elevation gain: up to 400 feet
     High point: 9,176 feet
     Hikable: mid-June through October
     Maps: USGS Bayhorse, Bayhorse Lake

Six kilns resembling dilapidated stone igloos sit near the old mining town of Bayhorse, built in the 1870s. Beyond Bayhorse a two-wheel-drive road leads 5 miles to Bayhorse Lake and to a short hike to Little Bayhorse Lake or a scenic scramble around Bayhorse Lake basin.

To reach the kilns, Bayhorse, and Bayhorse Lake, take Highway 75 north from Stanley 47 miles to the signed turnoff (road 051; 11 miles south of Challis). Cross the Salmon River and drive on road 051 up arid Bayhorse canyon 3.5 miles on good gravel road. You could mountain-bike this stretch. (The elevation gain is a noticeable 940 feet. Biking the next 5 miles to Bayhorse Lake, over 2,400 feet higher, is difficult.)

Historic Bayhorse, which is on patented land, was chosen in 1988 from 150 sites to be Idaho's Centennial Park. However, a purchase of the property from

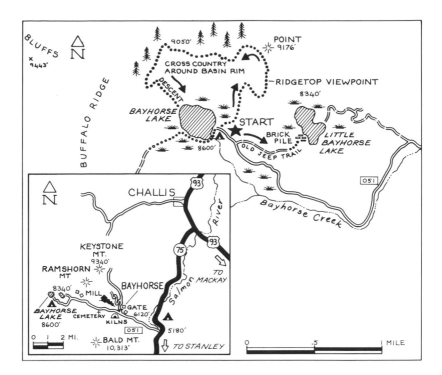

its owner did not come about, and the Centennial Park designation was given instead to Custer. As of 1989, a locked gate was at the entrance into Bayhorse's one main street and No Trespassing signs were posted. However, the kilns are alongside road 051 and can be inspected close up.

The kilns were used to turn wood into charcoal to feed the smelter, where high temperatures melted silver and lead from ore. Photos from two decades ago show the kilns intact, but now their domed rock ceilings have collapsed and stinging nettles guard the arched stone doorways. By the kilns the sprawling mill is in view across Bayhorse Creek on the north hillside. Check with the Yankee Fork Ranger District for updated information on Bayhorse.

Leaving the kilns for Bayhorse Lake, you'll pass a small graveyard 100 yards past the kilns. Farther up the canyon are more decrepit buildings, some teetering high on the steep, northern slope. At 3.3 miles from Bayhorse a rugged four-wheel-drive trail departs to Little Bayhorse Lake. Stay on the main road to reach the marshy shoreline of Bayhorse Lake and a Forest Service campground. A rowboat is helpful for fishing—no motors allowed.

For a 0.8-mile walk to Little Bayhorse Lake, take an old jeep road (now closed to vehicles) that begins in the meadow east of the Bayhorse Lake parking area. The road becomes a trail as it follows a gully and drops 260 feet in elevation to the smaller lake. In the mining heyday of over a century ago, brick

Bayhorse kiln

making was attempted here, and a pile of red crumbling bricks, intended to be used at Bayhorse, is near the shore.

Another hike from Bayhorse Lake is a challenging, 0.5-mile cross-country scramble, rising 400 feet to the ridge separating the two lakes. Begin by going northeast from Bayhorse Lake, across the large meadow, and continue among lodgepole pines to a talus slope. Climb through the rock and up the steep pitch to the ridge, where you'll overlook Little Bayhorse and Bayhorse canyon and see Bald Mountain filling the southeastern skyline. Retrace your steps to Bayhorse Lake or hike cross-country a mile around the rim of Bayhorse Lake basin. Look for Buffalo Ridge to the west, where rounded rock buttes appear like resting bison. Descend via one of several grass and gravel ravines back to the lake.

4 LOON CREEK–BEAVER CREEK ROAD

Best for: mountain biking
Opportunities for: scenic drive, hiking
39 miles one way
Moderate to difficult
Elevation gain: 3,600 feet; loss 5,800 feet
High point: 9,942 feet
Riding surface: dirt, gravel, rock
Ridable: mid-July through October
Maps: USGS Pinyon Peak, Casto, Knapp Lakes, Langer Peak;
    Forest Service 1:100,000 Frank Church–River of No Return
    Wilderness, south half

Pinyon Peak (9,942 feet) and Feltham Creek Point (9,000 feet) are connected by 7 miles of sky-high road atop a narrow ridge overlooking the largest wilderness area in the lower 48 states. The ridge road is part of a 39-mile route allowed to remain when the Frank Church–River of No Return Wilderness (FC-RNR) was established in 1980. A conditioned mountain biker can ride this road in a long day by using car support on two lengthy ascents. Consider also a weekend outing with a night's camp at Loon Creek. The trip begins either from Cape Horn or the Yankee Fork; the latter is described here, so the ridge ride is savored last.

If you take this trip as a scenic drive, the total loop distance is 95 miles. This includes 32 miles of pavement on Highway 75 and Highway 21; 14 miles on gravel roads; and 49 miles on more primitive road including the Loon Creek–Beaver Creek section, which requires high clearance and possibly four-wheel drive.

Some advice for a successful Loon Creek–Beaver Creek adventure: bring a support vehicle with enough room for all riders and bikes. Remember extra water and food. While uphill sections are stiff workouts, the brake-wearing downhill stretches are glorious fun—but with wreck potential. Watch for soft sand and loose gravel. Helmets are a must. Drivers need patience and mountain-proven cars to handle long, steep grades, hairpin turns, and eroded sections. Snow drifts can linger until midsummer. Check conditions first with Yankee Fork Ranger District.

From Stanley, take Highway 75 downriver 13 miles to Sunbeam, north up Yankee Fork Road 013 for 8.5 miles, passing the gold dredge, to Jordan Creek Road 172. A sign reads "River of No Return Wilderness, 9 miles; Loon Creek Guard Station, 20 miles." Unless you have thighs of steel, continue driving up mining-besieged Jordan Creek, passing Hecla Mining Company's massive, new open-pit gold mine. Be wary of heavy truck traffic. After 6 miles, start up seven rousing hairpin switchbacks to arrive 3 miles later at Loon Creek Summit (8,687 feet).

Whether driving or biking, catch your breath at Loon Creek Summit, where

Ready for a descent into Jordan Creek, the final leg of the Loon–Beaver ride

the wilderness boundary begins. Until exiting the wilderness 39 miles away on Beaver Creek Road, all motorized and mechanized travel is confined within 100 yards of the road. Bikers, tighten your helmets for two abrupt turns into the West Fork of Mayfield Creek, descending to Loon Creek Guard Station 11 miles away. The road eventually parallels the stream, bordered by a typical FC-RNR bear garden of wax currants, thimbleberries, roses, willows, and aspens. Primitive paths take off up China Creek and Mystery Creek.

Eight miles from Loon Creek Summit the East Fork of Mayfield Creek joins the West Fork. Look toward the bluffs across the stream for a startling skull face, its eyes and nose of black rock. A packtrail departs into the rough-and-tumble East Fork drainage. The hiking opportunities in the FC-RNR are beyond the scope of this book, but other authors have described them well. See Further Reading in the Appendices.

After three more miles, the confines of Mayfield Creek give way to fields along Loon Creek at the Forest Service guard station and private Diamond D Ranch (shown as Boyle Ranch on 1963 topo map). A mile past the guard station the road from Beaver Creek and Pinyon Creek joins Loon Creek. This is your route out of the canyon (for a side trip down Loon Creek, see below).

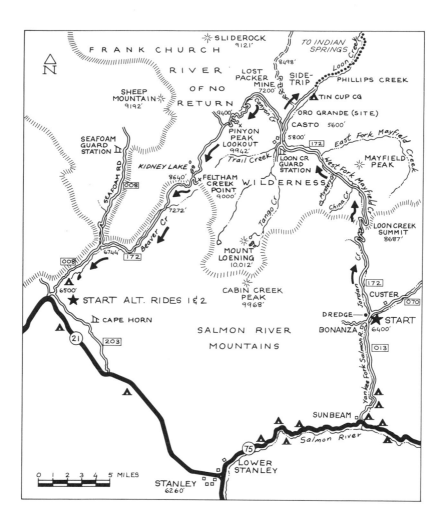

The base of Pinyon Peak is 9 miles away and 3,600 feet higher. (Another car-support segment for the non-endurance bikers.) On the way to Pinyon Peak you travel the hillside above Canyon Creek for 4 miles to Lost Packer Mine.

From the mine, the road twists 5 miles farther up Canyon Creek through a verdant, protected forest. At a crest (9,400 feet) see Pinyon Peak Lookout, a lonely lighthouse in a sea of mountains. A 1-mile trail leads to the lookout 542 feet higher.

The next 7 miles, to Feltham Creek Point, is what all the work has been for. It's a well-earned, high-altitude joy. Absorb the untrammeled views. To the northwest, wildlands drain toward the pristine Middle Fork of the Salmon River. Look for Sheep Mountain (9,192 feet) and Sliderock Mountain (9,121 feet). To the southeast, Trail Creek canyon drops more than 2,000 feet— almost from your tires in places. At times only the road occupies the skinny ridge top. Wide spots are sporadic.

As you near Feltham Creek Point, Kidney Lake lies 200 feet below in a basin to the north. Watch closely or you'll miss it. A fisherman's trail wanders down the steep hillside to the lake. Two smaller lakes are close by. The ridge ride is over when you reach the burned slope near the 0.5-mile, unmaintained side road to Feltham Creek Point, where the old lookout building is gone. With a few last hairpins, Beaver Creek Road tumbles 11 miles, sometimes viciously, to the wilderness perimeter and the junction with Seafoam Road 008. It's another five flat, but battering, washboard miles to Cape Horn Road 203 where a sign points to Highway 21, half a mile away. From there it's 19 miles east to Stanley.

Side Trip: Loon Creek to Phillips Creek Transfer Camp
10 miles round trip
Moderate
Elevation loss: 400 feet

Loon Creek Road continues 5 miles past the intersection with the Beaver Creek Road. At 1 mile is Casto, a stone house and a clutter of rusting machinery. Down the road, a historical sign marks Oro Grande (1869–1871), once a boom town of 1,500 optimistic miners.

At 2.5 miles, a four-wheel-drive road departs to Indian Springs Guard Station, 10 ragged, remote miles away. From the guard station, paths spoke out into wilderness heartland including Cougar Point, Little Loon Creek, and Loon Creek Lookout above the Middle Fork of the Salmon River. Past the Indian Springs turnoff, the Loon Creek Road goes by Loon Creek airstrip and on to Tin Cup Campground and Phillips Creek Transfer Camp at road's end. There wheels must stop, but feet and hooves walk on.

Alternative Ride 1: Loon Creek–Beaver Creek Road West to East (Cape Horn to Yankee Fork Gold Dredge)
53 miles one way
Moderate to difficult
Elevation gain: 5,800 feet, loss 5,887 feet

Once you've done the Loon Creek–Beaver Creek Road from the Yankee Fork to Cape Horn, try riding the reverse direction. The biking mileage begins at the junction of Cape Horn Road 203 and Seafoam Road 008. Pedaling from the Cape Horn area to Feltham Creek Point is arduous but possible. Once on the 7-mile ridge, you're mostly gaining elevation (800 feet) toward Pinyon Peak rather than resting. Wheeling down Canyon Creek to Loon Creek is an exhilarating flight, but then it's 11 miles and a 3,000-foot rise to Loon Creek Summit—time to climb aboard the shuttle van. From Loon Creek Summit the 9-mile descent into Jordan Creek is a screamer (watch for ore trucks and sandy roadbed). Once at the dredge, you've come 53 miles from Cape Horn. If that's not enough biking, coast another 8.5 miles down the Yankee Fork valley to Sunbeam Village and the Salmon River.

Coasting at 9,000 feet on the Loon–Beaver road

Alternative Ride 2: Cape Horn to Feltham Creek Point

      32 miles round trip
      Difficult
      Elevation gain: 2,140 feet

This round trip lets you sample the Beaver Creek–Loon Creek Road without needing a support vehicle (although you may wish for one toward the ascent's end). Start at the junction of Cape Horn Road 203 and Seafoam Road 008 and pedal 16 miles to the ridge near Feltham Creek Point, gaining 2,140 feet elevation. The ride is mild until the last 4 miles. That's when the road leaves Beaver Creek for Feltham Creek, enters rocky sections, and climbs more than 1,300 feet in a final stretch toward the base of Feltham Creek Point. Once there, stash your bike in the trees and hike 0.5 mile to the old lookout site for lunch.

5 NIP AND TUCK

Best for: mountain biking
Opportunities for: scenic drive, hiking
13-mile loop
Moderate
Elevation gain: 440 feet
High point: 6,640 feet
Riding surface: sand, gravel
Ridable: mid-May through October
Maps: USGS Stanley, Basin Butte, Elk Meadow

Turnaround at Stanley Creek Road

10.6 miles round trip
Moderate
Elevation gain: 440 feet

Nip and Tuck once was a "nip and tuck" jarring wagon way; now a nubby-tired bicycle rides easily on the dirt road. A few miles of uphill pedaling rewards with a Sawtooth panorama.

The description here focuses on mountain biking, but drivers, walkers, and picnickers can follow along and enjoy the views, too. (For a hike, see East

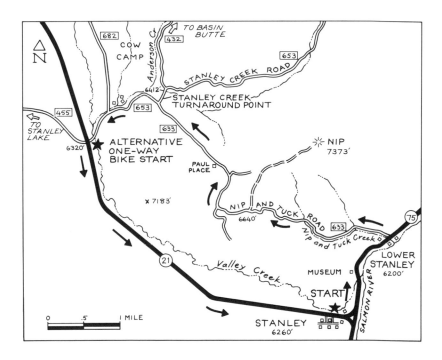

Fork Nip and Tuck Creek, trip 6.) During May, check locally first for road conditions—snow and mud may linger (more a problem for vehicles than bicyclists).

Half of the 13-mile loop trip is pavement (Highway 21). Highway-shunners can avoid the blacktop by making round trips on Nip and Tuck Road or taking the alternative one-way trip described below. The latter is suggested for families with youngsters. The full loop described here goes counterclockwise, beginning in Stanley, so there's over a mile of downhill "warm-up" riding before tackling Nip and Tuck's 440-foot elevation gain, followed by 9 miles of flat to downhill riding.

Ride Highway 75 (be careful of busy summer traffic) along the Salmon River, passing the old Stanley Ranger Station that's now a museum, for 1.2 miles to Lower Stanley. Nip and Tuck Road begins just past the village center. Look left (west) for a canyon and road 633 near what is presently (1989) the Middle Fork Rapid Transit Company headquarters.

The firm, dirt road climbs tamely through sagebrush for 0.8 mile to a culvert over the East Fork of Nip Creek. The creek flows from a canyon to the north (a nature walk awaiting discovery and described in trip 6).

Near 1.8 miles a knock-out view of the Sawtooths appears, including summits of Mount Heyburn, Horstman Peak, and Williams Peak. A jeep trail departs going left uphill and eventually links to Stanley.

At 2.8 miles, Nip and Tuck tops out at 6,640 feet. A barricaded, eroded track goes right, sharply uphill, along a fence. Foot travelers can follow it 1.6 miles to Nip Mountain. Nip and Tuck sails downward through woods, and as the road turns north, Red Mountain looms skyward in the Salmon River Mountains. Catch glimpses of Cabin Creek Peak to its left (west). At 3.8 miles, you're well into what's known as the Stanley Basin, and at the old "Paul Place," a fence protects roofless log walls. The road ahead is muddy early in the season, but meadows blaze with buttercups and marsh marigolds.

At 5.2 miles, reach a junction with Stanley Creek Road 653—probably signless, although marked by brown post and Forest Service bulletin board. This can be the turnaround point for the 10.6-mile round-trip ride. (Or explore farther up Stanley Creek or toward Anderson Gulch and Basin Butte.) To complete the Nip and Tuck loop, go straight (northwest) on washboard road. Across the meadow are three rustic log cabins. You'll also notice a maze of electric fence along meandering Stanley Creek, intended to keep cattle from breaking down streambanks. At certain times of year a large herd will accompany this ride. If you'd rather not dodge cowpies, check with the Stanley Ranger Station for the grazing schedule.

Just before Cow Camp turnoff at 6.2 miles is another picturesque homestead cabin. At 6.7 miles, reach Highway 21 and go left, riding east on pavement 5 miles to Stanley. Afternoon headwinds can be strong.

Alternative Ride: Stanley Creek Road–Nip and Tuck–Lower Stanley

> 6.5 miles one way
> Easy
> Elevation gain: 320 feet, loss 440 feet

Valley Creek near Stanley—a side trip from Nip and Tuck Road

An easier one-way ride begins 5 miles west of Stanley at the junction of Highway 21 and Stanley Creek Road 653 (opposite Stanley Lake Road). Ride the trip described above in reverse to Lower Stanley, 6.7 miles. Take time to explore. You'll need a car shuttle or an ambitious rider to go back to pick up the vehicle while the rest of the group suns by the river, patronizes eateries in Lower Stanley or Stanley, or perhaps visits the museum.

6 EAST FORK NIP AND TUCK CREEK

Best for: hiking
3 miles round trip
Easy to moderate
Elevation gain: 300 feet to 1,100 feet
High point: 7,373 feet
Hikable: May through October
Maps: USGS Stanley, Basin Butte

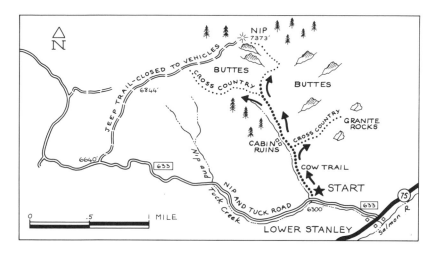

Late spring and early summer is the coolest and greenest time for this short walk that leads to many sights: two old cabins crumbling among Douglas firs; a scattering of statue-like rocks and massive buttes; and grand views of the Sawtooths on the ridge of Nip Mountain.

Follow directions in trip 5 (Nip and Tuck) for the first 0.8 mile up Nip and Tuck Road to the stream crossing. You're in the right place if you notice rusty cans at this former dumpsite and barricades to prevent motorcycles from climbing the nearby sage-covered hillsides. Follow a cow trail (there may be cows, many at times, so check beforehand at the Stanley Ranger Station to avoid the critters) along the creek's right side for 0.3 mile to a small tailings heap. Two fallen-in mining cabins are across the stream. On the northeast slope, look for sculpted granite projectiles in odd shapes, some resembling animals. A short, steep, off-trail hike of a few hundred yards permits closer inspection, climbing, and good photos. Be careful as you walk on the gravelly decomposing granite slope.

Another jaunt passes the tailings pile to where the drainage divides—look for a bedrock ridge between the two creek bottoms. Maneuver across the

47

boggy stream and climb the rock walkway upward 200 yards until it ends and sagebrush begins. You'll gain unobstructed views of the massive buttes in the upper canyon and a pleasant lunch site. Above to the north lies tree-covered Nip Mountain. To continue onward requires adventuresome spirit and willingness to declare your own route on game and cow trails.

By choosing a north-northwest direction up through bitterbrush and sage you'll gain the hilltop and see along the way a magnificent, unusual look at the Sawtooths—worth every uphill step. From the hilltop, a fence and jeep track lead to mossy, old-growth Douglas fir that have survived chainsaws. A rock-crib and post identifies the geological marker for Nip, 7,373 feet. At this point you've come about 1.5 miles from Nip and Tuck Road and gained nearly 1,100 feet in elevation. The buttes are now below to the southeast. From the backside, some of the massive rocks are a nontechnical, entertaining scramble, but beware of the precipitous frontsides, and keep youngsters in control.

Weather-sculpted granite rabbit in East Fork of Nip and Tuck Creek

7 JOE'S GULCH

Best for: mountain biking
Opportunities for: hiking
13.8-mile loop
Moderate to difficult
Elevation gain: 1,040 feet
High point: 7,000 feet
Riding surface: sand, dirt, gravel
Ridable: June through October
Maps: USGS Basin Butte, Stanley, Elk Meadow

Joe's Gulch contributes its share of sweaty brows as a winding link in the biking network nestled near Stanley in the Salmon River foothills. This loop trip combines Joe's Gulch and Nip and Tuck (trip 5). The eroded Joe's Gulch road is too rough for most vehicles. Hikers will enjoy the 2.5-mile walk from the Salmon River to the summit above the gulch, especially before summer heat bakes the canyon.

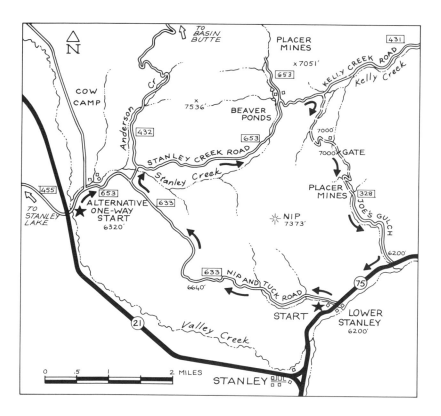

Mudhole in Joe's Gulch

Start in Lower Stanley, using directions for trip 5. Drive Nip and Tuck Road 4.9 miles to unsigned Stanley Creek Road 653. Turn right (north) on road 653 and go 0.3 mile to a signed junction with the Anderson Gulch–Basin Butte Road. Go right, following Stanley Creek, and pedal slightly upward through the Stanley Basin with the Sawtooths to the southwest for company. Red Mountain rises to the north. Pass beaver ponds as the valley narrows, and at 7.9 miles arrive at a Y. Your route is straight, on road 431, but it's worth a brief side trip to go left on Stanley Creek to see more impressive beaver work and a frontier cabin with a native stone fireplace.

Return to Kelly Creek Road (road 431) and climb a hill, reaching Joe's Gulch Road at 8.6 miles. Go right. The dirt surface is smooth pedaling until 9.3 miles when the gullied jeep trail starts sharply up to reach the first 7,000-foot summit. Unless the road has been repaired, biking is easier than driving.

At just over 10 miles, reach a second 7,000-foot-high point at a metal gate. Logging roads not shown on current maps lead in either direction along the ridge. From the gate, ride downhill into Joe's Gulch. As you approach the river the dry sagebrush slopes are brightened with scarlet gilia and, in late summer, the gold to reddish blossoms of sulphur plant. At 12.7 miles, reach Highway 75 and the Salmon River. Turn right and pedal a long mile back to Lower Stanley.

Alternative Ride: Stanley Creek to Joe's Gulch

> 10.3 miles one way
> Moderate
> Elevation gain: 680 feet, loss 800 feet

An easier ride skips Nip and Tuck Road and begins 5 miles west of Stanley on Highway 21 at road 653 to Stanley Creek. Pedal on road 653 for 1.5 miles and reach the intersection with Nip and Tuck Road. From this point follow the description above to Joe's Gulch. Since this is a one-way ride, you'll need to leave a car in Lower Stanley or have someone meet you there.

SAWTOOTH AND CHALLIS NATIONAL FORESTS

8 BASIN CREEK

> Best for: mountain biking
> Opportunities for: hiking
> 11.6 miles round trip
> Moderate
> Elevation gain: 420 feet
> High point: 6,480 feet
> Riding surface: primitive dirt road
> Ridable: June through October
> Maps: USGS Basin Butte, East Basin Creek

Forested Basin Creek canyon is a shady ride on a warm summer day or an early-season choice when higher elevations are still blocked by snow. Bike or

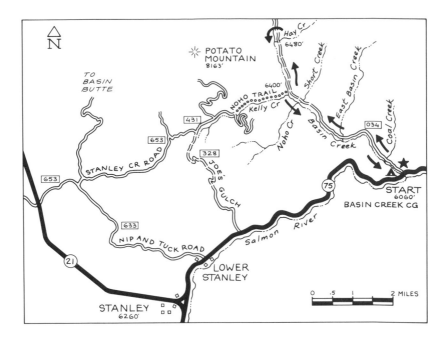

Beaver dam on Basin Creek

Monkeyflower

hike early morning or evening to see deer and other wildlife.

Start at Basin Creek Campground, 8.3 miles from Stanley on Highway 75. Basin Creek Road is a high-clearance, primitive route that immediately climbs a buckwheat-covered hillside above the stream and then levels as it passes Coal Creek at 0.6 mile. At 1.2 miles, pedal another hill (take heart—the trip back will be a free-wheeling coast).

At 2.3 miles, the road crosses East Basin Creek and becomes hummocky as it weaves through the canyon, passing meadows, willow thickets, and beaver ponds. Mudhole fans will find plenty of splattering in June. At 3.8 miles, Short Creek enters from the right (north) and Noho Creek drainage is seen to the distant south. At 4.2 miles, just before a slight hill, pass the unsigned and easy-to-miss turnoff for the Noho Trail (trip 9) across Basin Creek. (The Noho Trail goes along Kelly Creek, not Noho Creek. This is Idaho, folks!) Continue riding up Basin Creek Road, passing a stock gate near Hay Creek at 5.7 miles. Reach a hunting camp by a stream ford at 5.8 miles—the turnaround point. Or continue biking the rough packtrail with its numerous crossings of Basin Creek. The trail eventually leads to Hindman Lake, 7 miles away. *Note:* The last few miles of Basin Creek road is slated to be closed to vehicles and rehabilitated. Future trail reconstruction is also planned.

Coasting by a beaver pond on Stanley Creek

9 NOHO TRAIL

Best for: mountain biking
12.3 miles one way
Moderate (stream crossing)
Elevation gain: 440 feet; loss 700 feet
High point: 6,760 feet
Riding surface: gravel and dirt road, primitive trail
Ridable: late June through October
Maps: USGS Basin Butte, East Basin Butte

Noho Trail is an abandoned road that becomes a challenging trail near Basin Creek, a main tributary to the Salmon River. Taking this ride too early (May to mid-June), before spring runoff subsides, brings shouts of "oh no, Noho," as you stand on Basin Creek's banks and yearn for the short route home on the opposite shore.

A one-way ride begins 5 miles west of Stanley Creek Road 653 (opposite

Stanley Lake turnoff). Have someone drop you off here and meet you at trip's end at Basin Creek Campground by the Salmon River, or shuttle a car to Basin Creek. Follow road 653, bypassing at 1.4 miles the unsigned junction with Nip and Tuck Road. At 1.7 miles, reach the Basin Butte–Anderson Gulch intersection. Go right, continuing gradually upward through the Stanley Basin on road 653, and at 4.4 miles, go straight, uphill, on Kelly Creek Road 431. At 5.1 miles, pass Joe's Gulch jeep trail and at 5.4 miles, watch for a reservoir just before the placer diggings near the old Starkey cabins.

Coast into Kelly Creek, passing a high-standard logging road 065 at 5.6 miles (which winds for more than two scenic miles with Sawtooth views up the southern slopes of Potato Mountain). At 6.2 miles, pass Sawmill Creek (where a primitive road dead-ends in 0.3 mile). At 6.4 miles, leave Kelly Creek Road, go around a barricade preventing vehicle access, and follow the Noho Trail down Kelly Creek. (If you start going uphill on a right-hand turn, you missed the cutoff.) For a mile the Noho Trail route is mostly along an old road, turning to a path for the next 0.4 mile that requires clever riding as it traverses above and through Kelly Creek. Unless the trail's been recently maintained, you'll likely have to hop over deadfall. At just over 8 miles, reach Basin Creek— a 30-foot-wide stream that's a foot deep, even in late summer. Ride if you dare. Otherwise, shoulder your bike and wade across.

Go right, following Basin Creek on the primitive Basin Creek Road 034 for 4.2 miles through the wooded canyon to a waiting car at Basin Creek Campground near the Salmon River and Highway 75. From Basin Creek Campground, it's 8.3 miles upriver to Stanley via Highway 75.

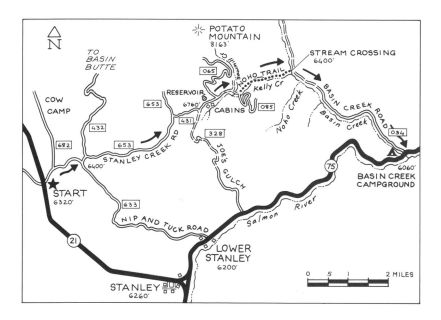

10 BASIN BUTTE LOOKOUT

Best for: mountain biking
Opportunities for: scenic drive, hiking
16.6 miles round trip
Difficult
Elevation gain: 2,442 feet
High point: 8,854 feet
Riding surface: dirt road
Ridable: July through October
Map: USGS Basin Butte

Alternative Ride: Basin Butte

8.3 miles one way
Easy
Elevation loss: 2,442 feet

Turnaround above Anderson Gulch

5.8 miles round trip
Moderate
Elevation gain: 600 feet
Ridable: June through October

Halloween day bike ride on Basin Butte road

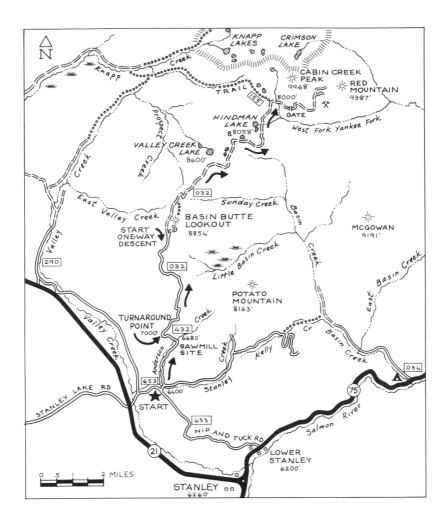

The faraway spires of Cabin Creek Peak (9,968 feet) are visible on the northern skyline when driving along the Salmon River just past the Stanley Ranger Station, 3 miles from Stanley.

This outing takes you to Basin Butte Lookout, which lies en route to Hindman Lake and nearby Cabin Creek Peak (trip 11).

While Cabin Creek Peak is more visible, closer Basin Butte Lookout is far more visited, a fact related to the wild and woolly nature of the road once beyond Basin Butte. A bicycling trip to either is difficult without a support car.

By driving the steep climb (high clearance and four-wheel drive helpful) to Basin Butte and having a shuttle driver leave you and your bike at the lookout, you can coast back to the valley floor.

Basin Butte is reached from Stanley, going west on Highway 21 to Stanley

Western groundsel—one of the most common Sawtooth Country wildflowers

Creek Road 653 (opposite Stanley Lake Road). Go 1.4 miles on road 653 to a junction with unsigned Nip and Tuck Road and park. Biking mileage begins here. At 0.3 mile, at a T intersection, go left on road 432 (which eventually becomes road 032) toward Anderson Gulch and Basin Butte. The sign says "Basin Butte 10 miles," but actual distance is 8 miles.

If you're pedaling, enjoy the tame miles along Anderson Creek, passing an old sawmill site at Anderson Gulch at 2 miles, which signals the start of harder biking. At 2.9 miles, pause by an old logging trail for a wide view of the Stanley Basin, distant Stanley Lake, and the Sawtooths. This overlook can be a picnic destination and turnaround point for a shorter ride.

The road to Basin Butte continues its steady uphill grind, with a few level stretches interspersed, before reaching the signed Basin Butte access road at 7.6 miles. At 8.3 miles is the lookout, an elevation gain of 2,442 feet. The last 0.7 mile has one breath-taking moment—a rutted, eroded, hairpin turn on the mountainside.

Atop Basin Butte you'll receive a geography primer of the Sawtooths, Sawtooth Valley, Stanley Basin, White Clouds, and Salmon River Mountains. Look for Little Basin Creek Meadows and Potato Mountain 2 miles below to the southeast. To the northeast is the top half of Cabin Creek Peak. When you're ready to leave, coast back on roads 032 and 432 to your start in the Stanley Basin.

11 HINDMAN LAKE, CABIN CREEK PEAK

Best for: mountain biking
Opportunities for: hiking, scenic drive
18 miles round trip
Difficult
Elevation gain: continuous ascents and descents
Riding surface: primitive, 4WD dirt and rock road
Ridable: July through mid-October
Maps: USGS Basin Butte, Knapp Lakes

This trip begins from the junction of Hindman Lake–Cabin Creek Peak Road 032 and the access road to Basin Butte Lookout (read trip 10 for directions and background).

Driving from Basin Butte to Hindman Lake and Cabin Creek Peak is its own adventure. Biking is strenuous, but far less harrowing than driving. For pedaling, bring a support vehicle with an experienced mountain driver and start early or plan an overnighter at the lake. For most bikers, a one-way ride

The road to Cabin Creek Peak is a mean one.

On the road to Cabin Creek Peak

into Hindman Lake is enough (and perhaps descending the final 8.3 miles from Basin Butte, described in trip 10, on the return).

The four-wheel-drive route ahead, especially the last 4 miles to Hindman Lake, is among central Idaho's most exciting and treacherous as the narrow road leads in and out of steep canyons. Despite the condition of the road, many recreationists with steady nerves use it. Since trees are commonly blown down across the road, come prepared with a saw or ax. Also, on stormy days be wary of tumbling rocks and water runoff from the erosion-prone hillsides.

After the junction for Basin Butte Lookout, the Hindman Lake Road traverses the hillsides above East Valley Creek canyon, then zigzags eastward above Sunday Creek. At 3.5 miles, driving intensifies as the track clings to the mountainside. At 3.9 miles, a campsite on the road's north side marks a well-beaten path to Valley Creek Lake, over the north ridge and 550 feet lower.

At 4.6 miles is a partial view of Cabin Creek Peak, just before a chilling descent that leads to two peaceful, flower-lined ponds. Another larger lakelet is at 6 miles. At 7.1 miles, pass the start of Basin Creek trail, and at 7.3 miles, in a clearing, is a full view of Cabin Creek Peak. At 7.5 miles, you'll happily see the green shoreline of Hindman Lake appear. Walk around the lake's left (south) shore for an unobstructed look at Cabin Creek Peak to the northeast.

Past the trodden-in shores of Hindman, the road continues to Knapp Lakes trail 155, at 8.7 miles. At 9 miles, the road is gated to stop traffic from continuing toward Red Mountain (aptly named) where active mining claims exist.

For hikers there's exploring aplenty either along the signed Knapp Lakes trail or on a forested cross-country route toward the goat ledges on Cabin Creek Peak's southwest face. Use the Knapp Lakes topo to locate unnamed lakes.

CHALLIS NATIONAL FOREST

12 BLIND SUMMIT

Best for: mountain biking
Opportunities for: scenic drive
16-mile loop
Moderate
Elevation gain: 263 feet
High point: 6,903 feet
Riding surface: dirt and gravel roads, 1.2 miles pavement
Ridable: late May through October
Maps: USGS Elk Meadow, Banner Summit, Langer Peak

Turnaround at Knapp Creek Sheep Bridge
10 miles round trip
Easy
Elevation loss: 32 feet

Blind Summit lies in the Cape Horn region northwest of Stanley, an area of low-wooded foothills, backcountry dirt roads, and miles of meadowlands, nourished by a threadwork of small streams feeding Marsh Creek.

In this area and trip 13, watch for bands of sheep and their guard dogs. If possible, skirt the flock, or look for the sheep herder and ask him to call his dogs so that you can pass through the band without incident.

From Stanley city limits, drive northwest on Highway 21. Notice Valley Creek Road 290 at 9.8 miles, your exit on the loop ride. At 11 miles from Stanley, turn onto Cape Horn Road 203 and park. It's 0.8 mile to a carved wooden sign identifying and explaining Blind Summit. The riding is easy and mostly smooth on a firm, gravel surface—unless log trucks are hauling, then the road may have washboard sections.

At 5 miles, just before road 203 bridges Knapp Creek near the Cape Horn

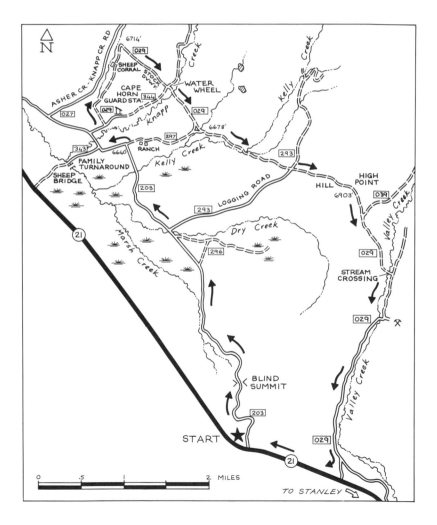

Power-pedal letdown—crossing Valley Creek. A bridge is planned.

Guard Station turnoff, look for "Short-Cut" road 343 going left. This signals the turnaround point for a shorter ride. Take road 343 for 0.2 mile to a sheep bridge over Marsh Creek. Lunch by the stream with expansive views of meadows and mountains. In August you may see spawning salmon—watch quietly, without disturbing these rare fish. (A family ride could end here; the kids can play while one adult goes back to retrieve the car.)

To continue the loop ride, stay on road 203 until the Cape Horn Guard Station–Asher Creek Sheep Corral Road at 5.2 miles. Go right. In 0.1 mile, at the guard station gate, go left along a log worm fence on a primitive road that leads to the corrals at 6.2 miles. Continue past the corrals and watch at 6.5 miles for a stock driveway going right. Cross a culvert over an irrigation stream by a waterwheel at 7.3 miles. At 7.5 miles, cross Knapp Creek. You're going east, following road 029. At 7.9 miles, bypass road 297 (a potential shortcut which leads south a mile back to Cape Horn Road 203). At 8.1 miles, pass another fork of road 297.

Continue riding east on road 029 and gently climb through dry clearings with views to the south of Copper Mountain. At 9.3 miles, bypass logging road 293 (its right branch connects in 1.7 miles back to Cape Horn Road 203 near Dry Creek). Pedal uphill for the next long mile on soft gravel until topping out in forest at 6,903 feet. At 10.4 miles, at a T intersection, go right, following the powerline. Soon the road drops rapidly into Valley Creek meadows. At 10.8

Biking Cape Horn Road on a windy late summer day

miles, pass inviting trail 039 going left up Valley Creek canyon (described in trip 13, Valley Creek–Knapp Creek). Today's route continues coasting downstream until halted by a crossing of Valley Creek at 11.7 miles. A bridge is planned in 1995 in order to protect salmon spawning beds. Please use the bridge, especially during July, August, and September when salmon may be present.

The stream bottom is compacted coarse sand and odds are 50/50 you'll go shore to shore standing up—but never dry. In high water, use a log jam downstream. After the crossing, follow road 029 and reach Highway 21 at 14.5 miles. Turn right and go with summer traffic another 1.2 miles to your car at Cape Horn Road.

13 VALLEY CREEK, KNAPP CREEK

Best for: mountain biking
25.3-mile loop
Moderate
Elevation gain: 1,120 feet
High point: 7,200 feet
Riding surface: dirt roads and trails
Ridable: mid-June through October
Maps: USGS Elk Meadow, Langer Peak, Knapp Lakes

Turnaround at Valley Creek Crossing
5.6 miles round trip
Easy
Elevation gain: 148 feet

A loop ride along Valley and Knapp creeks is supreme biking on agreeable
firm roads and trails; just enough cobbles and climbing for interest, stream
crossings and mudholes for spice. Come around July 4th to see miles of mead-

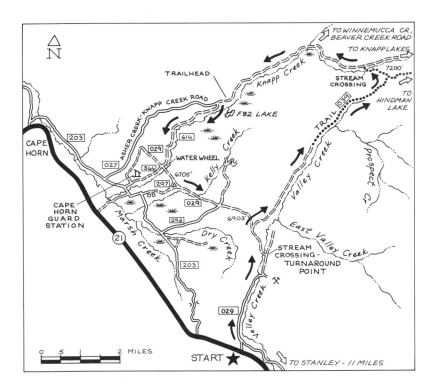

owlands ablaze with wildflowers. Depart early morning to see elk—and come before October hunting.

On a map, the loop appears simple, but on-going road and trail changes, plus rounded, rolling terrain without landmarks, can be perplexing. It's helpful to take the Elk Meadow and Langer Peak topos and a Challis forest map. Also, read or ride trip 12 (Blind Summit) for an introduction to Cape Horn—this loop repeats 7 miles of that trip. This trip can also be shortened by using two cars (leave one in Valley Creek by Highway 21 and one near Cape Horn Guard Station).

The 1994 Challis Forest Travel Plan map incorrectly shows the entire Valley Creek–Knapp Creek route as open to all-terrain vehicles (four-wheelers). As of 1994, Valley Creek trail 039 was impassable to these machines and no trail reconstruction is planned in the near future.

Drive northwest of Stanley's city limits on Highway 21 for 9.8 miles to Valley Creek Road 029. Go through a stock gate and park. Pedal gradually up Valley Creek canyon on the loop's only washboards and go right at 0.5 mile, crossing Valley Creek on a stout wooden bridge. At 2.3 miles, pass Valley Creek mine road, continuing straight, following a powerline, past a log worm fence at 2.4 miles. Valley Creek flows through lush vegetation as you approach a sign at 2.8 miles pointing left: "Stock Driveway, Knapp Creek 4." Go left 200 yards on rutted road 029 to a ford of Valley Creek (a new bridge is planned to protect salmon spawning habitat—please use the bridge if completed!).

This can be the turnaround point for families. You can picnic or loll along the stream, or explore up East Valley Creek road for a mile. In August you

Lake F82 is a short cross-country walk from the Knapp Creek trailhead.

may see spawning salmon. Keep your distance and observe quietly; these magnificent fish are endangered. To continue the loop, cross Valley Creek, following road 029 to a meadow at mile 3.7. Look for trail 039 leading right and follow it, leaving the powerline road (road 029). (The loop ride returns to this point 21.6 miles into the trip.) Ride easily through lodgepole forest and more meadows along Valley Creek. In later summer the appealing scene is well worn by grazing (true of all the route ahead).

After 7 miles the primitive road becomes a trail, turning rocky and hilly at times, and passing an old sign for Prospect Creek at 8.9 miles. Now gear down and lower your bike seat for the next 0.5 mile along a hillside that's steep and root strewn. Maybe it's time to give in and dismount. At 9.6 miles, reach a T junction (different than the four-way junction shown on 1964 Knapp Lake topo map) where a sign reads: "Hindman Lake 6, Cape Horn Guard Station 10." Go left. Your route is toward Cape Horn.

After briefly climbing, at 9.8 miles descend over a tree-root staircase to Knapp Creek at 10.2 miles. Search for the driest ford—the stream is almost ridable by July. Slog through a willow thicket and reach a jeep road at 10.2 miles. Three signs point to various destinations; go left, toward Cape Horn. At 11 miles, a highpoint brings a view of the surrounding forested countryside. At 11.8 miles, after zooming downhill, meet an ankle-deep, gooey mudhole. Another up and down and at 12.4 miles, reach another sign near an eroded, dry streambed. Cross the ditch and go left, riding on road 027 down Knapp Creek, through acres of blossoms in June. The overgrown road is closed to vehicles by three tanktraps you'll soon encounter—skirt the bulldozed dirt humps. At 15.4 miles, reach the Knapp Creek trailhead.

After the trailhead, it's 0.4 mile to a very faint track going left through a clearing. *Watch closely*—this is your scenic shortcut home. (The main road is shown on Forest Service maps, but not on the 1972 topo; it follows Asher Creek to reach Cape Horn Road 203. This new road is called Asher Creek–Knapp Creek Road—road 027.) In 100 yards you'll encounter a distinct road. You're now riding the old, abandoned Knapp Creek Road 614 shown on the 1972 Langer Peak topo, but not on current forest maps. At 16.3 miles, the road dims as it enters a mile-long meadow. The overgrown, rutted track becomes a one-lane, foot-deep furrow that barely allows pedaling. At 17.5 miles, climb sharply 200 yards over a ridge and gain splendid views of the Sawtooths and Cape Horn country. Then careen off the ridge and, at 18.2 miles, reach a crossroads near a waterwheel and culvert on an irrigation canal. Go left. Don't miss this turn!

(A right turn on road 029 goes 1 mile to Asher Creek sheep corrals and another mile to Cape Horn Road 203. Straight ahead road 344 leads through two gates and goes 1.2 miles to Cape Horn Guard Station and road 203. A loop ride could be shortened (by 5 to 6 miles) and made easier by leaving a second car at Cape Horn Road 203 near the guard station turnoff.)

Cross the canal and, in 18.4 miles, cross Knapp Creek by bridge. You're riding due east on road 029 (until signs were changed in 1995, this route was confusingly signed on the ground as road 290).

Continue heading due east, back toward Valley Creek, ignoring side roads. At 21.2 miles, after a mile-long climb on soft gravel, reach an intersection. Go straight, following the powerline. At last, drop into Valley Creek, back to the stream crossing at 22.5 miles, and breeze the final downhill stretch to your car at 25.3 miles.

CHALLIS NATIONAL FOREST

Frank Church–River of No Return Wilderness

14 MARSH CREEK, BIG HOLE, DAGGER FALLS

Best for: hiking
10 miles to 30 miles round trip
Easy
Elevation loss: 240 feet
High point: 6,440 feet
Hikable: June through October
Maps: USGS Cape Horn Lakes; Forest Service 1:100,000
    Frank Church–River of No Return Wilderness, south half

Alternative Hike: Marsh Creek to Dagger Falls

15 miles one way
Moderate
Elevation loss: 880 feet
Maps: USGS Cape Horn Lakes, Greyhound Ridge,
    Chinook Mountain SE

The packbridge a mile below Marsh Creek transfer camp, a family short hike destination

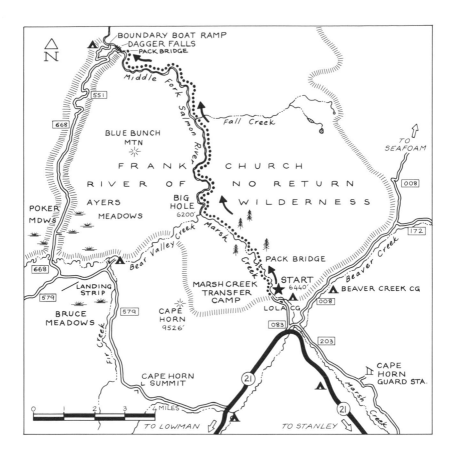

Drive along the Salmon River downstream from Stanley and envision it 150 years ago—untamed, roadless. Marsh Creek in the Frank Church–River of No Return Wilderness remains such a place. More a river than mere creek, Marsh Creek flows through a mildly wild and ever-deepening forested canyon. Wander here for a mile or hike 5 miles to Big Hole or 15 miles to Dagger Falls.

From Stanley, drive 18.6 miles northwest on Highway 21 past the northern Sawtooths and Vader Meadows. Turn right on road 083 and follow signs for Lola Campground and Middle Fork trail (also called Marsh Creek trail for its first 15 miles). Road 083 reaches Marsh Creek transfer camp in 1.5 miles. Stern warnings against mountain bike use on the Marsh Creek trail are posted.

The trail begins away from the creek, passes a talus village of pikas, and winds through berries and blossoms, beneath pines with scurrying chipmunks and squirrels. The path comes close to water's edge just before Collie Creek at 1 mile. A few hundred yards beyond, a sturdy stock bridge spans Marsh Creek. Choose the bridge as a short (1.2 miles) hiking goal with detours on fishermen's

Dagger Falls during September flow

paths to investigate the river close up. There's no getting lost on Marsh Creek, but adults with children should take care near its turbulent stretches.

Past the stock bridge, a narrow, sloughing, hillside traverse, which enabled foot travelers to feel brave but was too exciting for horses and mules, was scheduled to be widened in 1989–90 (check with Yankee Fork Ranger District for an update; other improvements were also planned farther downstream). For most day hikers the destination is Big Hole, a deep pool just below the confluence of Bear Valley Creek and Marsh Creek. The 5-mile walk loses only 240 feet elevation, so the return upriver is fairly flat, though often warm—bring drinking water.

Big Hole is not seen from Marsh Creek trail. Look for side trails leading toward the river once Bear Valley Creek canyon appears to the west. You're close when you pass several sandy, overused campsites. A rock point conveniently overlooks the dark green swirls of Big Hole.

When Bear Valley Creek and Marsh Creek merge they become Idaho's most famous white-water river: the Middle Fork of the Salmon. From Big

Big Hole on Marsh Creek

Hole downstream, the Middle Fork flows 106 miles as a National Wild River through wilderness. Before a road was built to Dagger Falls in the 1950s and a boat ramp was constructed at nearby Boundary Creek, river runners in wooden boats (and later on, rubber rafts) put in at Bear Valley Creek in high water. They floated to Marsh Creek and on to Dagger Falls, portaged the drop, and continued down the Middle Fork. Today, early in the season, experienced kayakers run Marsh Creek or Bear Valley Creek, watching warily for logs.

The Marsh Creek trail continues past Big Hole for 10 more miles, climbing in and out of tributary streams, to reach the campground at Dagger Falls. Arrange to meet a car there and you can walk the trail in a day. River shuttle companies in Stanley will take your vehicle to Dagger Falls.

(To drive to Dagger Falls, take Highway 21 west of Stanley for 22 miles to gravel road 579 and a sign for Boundary Creek. Go right and drive 20 miles, following signs to the falls. During June and July, road 579 bustles with river-bound traffic.)

■ Sawtooth Mountains ■

Northern Sawtooths

SAWTOOTH NATIONAL FOREST
Sawtooth National Recreation Area
Sawtooth Wilderness

15 IRON CREEK, SAWTOOTH LAKE

Best for: hiking
10 miles round trip
Moderate
Elevation gain: 1,720 feet
High point: 8,430 feet
Hikable: mid-July through October
Map: USGS Stanley Lake

Turnaround at Iron Creek Meadow
2.4 miles round trip
Easy
Elevation gain: 300 feet
Hikable: June through October

Decades of contented hikers have worn a sunken trail to 173-acre Sawtooth Lake, the Sawtooth Wilderness's largest. Winds whip across the 250-foot-deep lake, buffeting the rocky shoreline. The shadowed north face of Mount Regan (10,190 feet) towers over it. By Idaho standards the route is crowded, 50 hikers or more on a summer weekend day. Along the trail you'll pass Alpine Lake, where there's calmer camping and safer roaming for children. (Another Alpine Lake is in Redfish canyon; see trip 26).

Access to Sawtooth Lake is quick from Stanley. Drive 2.5 miles west on Highway 21 to Iron Creek Road 619. Continue three dusty, bumpy miles to Iron Creek trailhead. A sign warns of *No Campfires* at Sawtooth or Alpine lakes due to scarce wood and fragile soil. The path begins in lodgepole forest, crosses the wilderness boundary, and meets the Alpine Way trail at 1.2 miles. Iron Creek is nearby, meandering crystal clear through alpine gardens. A short, soothing walk can end here.

Turn right on Alpine Way trail, going 0.6 mile to another junction. Turn left, leaving the Alpine Way trail, which continues northwest to Stanley Lake. The Sawtooth Lake trail climbs through forested switchbacks and reaches a stream crossing on rocks or logs at 3 miles. On the creek's south shore lies a

Sawtooth Lake and Mount Regan

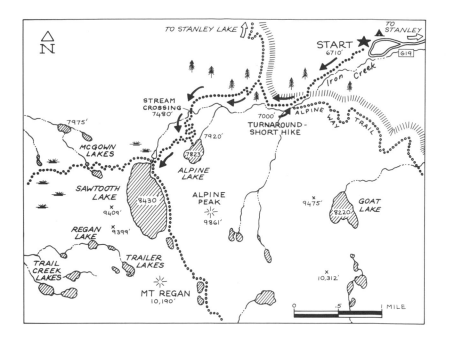

Sign along Iron Creek

large boulder where many a hiker has rested before facing the 0.8-mile climb (and 450-foot gain in elevation) to Alpine Lake ridge. At 3.8 miles, the lake lies below to the east, a few hundred yards by path. Sawtooth Lake is another mile beyond and 500 feet higher on a breathless, wondrous trail chiseled from rock.

The path becomes tame upon reaching the outlet stream and tundra ponds before the lake at 4.8 miles. Go left 0.25 mile farther for a sheltered lunch perch on the granite above the shoreline.

With its high visitor count and scarcity of campsites (the available sites are closer to the water than regulations are supposed to permit), Sawtooth Lake should be a day-hike destination. Nearby pools have flat lawns, but the fragile turf will suffer under boots and tents. To spend the night, move on 1.5 miles toward McGown Lakes or continue Sawtooth Lake's length to the North Fork Baron Creek canyon. The latter region has unnamed lakes and unwritten rewards awaiting.

For a compelling photo of Sawtooth Lake and Mount Regan take a late afternoon walk a half-mile and 300 feet up to the west ridge using the McGown Lake trail.

SAWTOOTH NATIONAL FOREST
Sawtooth National Recreation Area

16 ELK MOUNTAIN, ELK MEADOW

Best for: mountain biking
Opportunities for: hiking
12.4-mile loop
Moderate
Elevation gain: 500 feet
High point: 7,674 feet
Riding surface: gravel and dirt roads; rocky trail
Ridable: mid-June through October
Maps: USGS Stanley Lake, Elk Meadow

Hiking Turnaround at Elk Meadow
2.8 miles round trip
Easy
Elevation loss: 285 feet

From Stanley Lake, view stunning McGown Peak (9,860 feet). Above the lake's northern shore rises Elk Mountain, unobtrusive and unnoticed. A gravel logging road climbs Elk Mountain's eastern ridge and is part of a signed loop developed in 1989 by the Sawtooth Forest for mountain bikers, motorbikers, and horsemen. Once this loop had two exciting crossings of Elk Creek, but one crossing is now bridged and new trail construction planned in 1995 will eliminate the second.

To reach Stanley Lake, drive 5 miles west of Stanley on Highway 21 and turn left on Stanley Lake Road 455. After 3 miles of the bumpiest washboards

McGown Peak as seen from final miles of Elk Mountain–Elk Meadow loop

in Sawtooth land (improvements are promised) reach the lake—a favorite of car campers and powerboaters. Continue another 0.5 mile to the signed Elk Mountain Road 649 and parking area. If you're biking, stretch your legs for 1.9 miles of hard climbing, gaining 500 feet elevation to the hiker trailhead and registration box for trail 629 to Elk Meadow.

(Before taking Elk Meadow trail continue up the two-wheel-drive road for another 1.3 miles—a strenuous pedal—to road's end and an overlook of McGown Peak.)

The path descends through forest for 1.4 miles on cobbles and roots—technical riding. Challenge your friends to ride this boulder-boulevard clean (not touching a foot to the ground). After clanging pedals on the boulders, tree roots become the next obstacles—a gripping ride. At 3.3 miles reach Elk Meadow.

For hikers the meadows and winding channels of brooklike Elk Creek are usually the destination, enhanced by wildflowers in June and glowing sunsets over the northern Sawtooths. The trail through the meadow shown on the 1972 topo is more imagination than fact, lost in marsh and elk hoofprints.

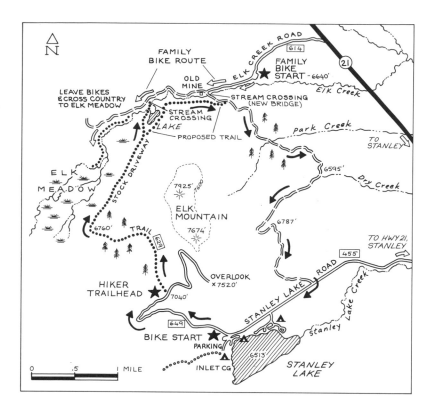

The loop trail route goes right, almost immediately leaving the meadow and following an old stock driveway. At 4.9 miles, a shallow lake nearly hidden by the lodgepole forest invites a swim. (Near this point a new trail is planned for 1995 construction. The new route will go along the hillside south of the lake and Elk Creek.)

At 5.1 miles, pass a log fence just before Elk Creek. Wade the stream, go 200 yards on a game trail and join hummocky Elk Meadow Road at 5.2 miles. Go right on the roller-coaster surface that's excellent riding until turning to cobbles near an old mine at 6.1 miles. Turn right at the mine and cross Elk Creek on a new bridge. (Once the new trail is built, the ford of Elk Creek, riding Elk Meadow Road, and crossing the new bridge by the mine will be optional.)

Once over Elk Creek, push your bike up a steep mining road, skirting old prospects, and reach easier pedaling at 6.4 miles, as the jeep trail winds pleasantly through cut clearings and Hereford-grazed meadows for the next several miles. At 10.3 miles, just before a long downgrade, is an outstanding look at regal McGown Peak. Backroad riding ends at Stanley Lake Road at 11 miles. Go right, slightly up a "phantom hill" for a mile (it looks down, but isn't) and reach trip's end at 12.4 miles.

Alternative Ride: Elk Creek Road to Elk Meadow

3 miles round trip
Easy
Elevation gain: 80 feet

This scenic 3-mile round-trip family ride is easier on muscles and equipment than the Elk Mountain loop. From Stanley, drive 8.5 miles to graveled road 614. Riding can begin here on the washboard road, but it's easier on children to keep driving 1.3 miles to a large pullout above Elk Creek. From the turnout, pedal up the increasingly primitive road (good riding) passing the old mine in 0.5 mile and reaching a sign for the Elk Mountain loop trail at 1.4 miles. Stay right, following the road, crossing a rocky washout, to a log fence above Elk Creek at 1.6 miles. Hide your bikes in the woods and walk down to Elk Creek, following it upstream 0.2 mile to the start of 2-mile-long Elk Meadow. Explore and linger in this special, rare landform. And remember to bring insect repellent!

SAWTOOTH NATIONAL FOREST
Sawtooth National Recreation Area

17 LADY FACE AND BRIDAL VEIL FALLS

Best for: hiking
6.8 miles round trip
Easy
Elevation gain: 320 feet
High point: 6,840 feet
Hikable: late June through October
Map: USGS Stanley Lake

Turnaround at Lady Face Falls

4.4 miles round trip
Easy to moderate (cross-country section)
Elevation gain: 280 feet

An easy outing with two surmountable challenges leads up Stanley Lake Creek canyon for 2.2 miles to Lady Face Falls and continues another 1.2 miles to Bridal Veil Falls. The first challenge is finding Lady Face Falls (it's off the trail a short distance). The second is wading Stanley Lake Creek on the way to Bridal Veil Falls.

Begin near Stanley Lake Inlet Campground (see trip 16 for access). Pass through a wooden stock gate. The first mile is a stroll through mountain meadows.

Granite chasm above Lady Face Falls

The scented walk through fields of larkspur, cinquefoil, and penstemon may include stepping aside for motorbikes, at least until Bridal Veil Falls. This may change, since the Sawtooth Forest has recommended Stanley Lake Creek to be added to the Sawtooth Wilderness.

After 1.1 miles, reach a junction with Alpine Way; continue straight (west). At 1.9 miles, the trail ascends a rocky hill, bends left through trees swept down by avalanche, and turns right (south) at 2.1 miles. Here a sign (easy to miss because it faces south) points to a faint, unofficial path that leads cross-country 250 yards through forest to a granite chasm containing a series of cascades and the 30-foot drop of Lady Face Falls. You'll hear the pounding water before seeing it. WARNING: Keep youngsters tightly in hand and be extremely cautious. The banks above the falls are steep, slippery, and potentially dangerous.

Hikers on the Stanley Lake Creek trail

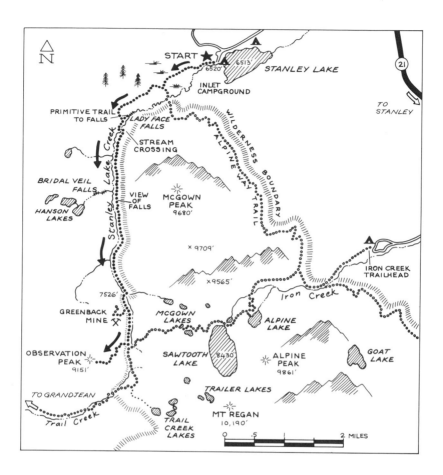

At Lady Face Falls in June and July, Stanley Lake Creek churns wickedly through the narrow ravine. In August, clear pools form between rapids. A full view of the waterfall is obstructed by trees and rock. The safest watching and sitting is upstream from the falls, where the drop-off is less precipitous.

Most hikers bypass the adventurous route to Lady Face and head to Bridal Veil Falls. At 2.4 miles the trail (once an old road to the Greenback Mine) crosses Stanley Lake Creek. Wade or use a logjam—early in the season water is thigh deep here.

At 3.3 miles, distant Bridal Veil Falls cascades down the west mountain-side, fed from Hanson Lakes 1,000 feet above. At 3.4 miles, just after a sign closing the trail ahead to motorbikes, is a clear view of the distant falls. Paths head toward the falls, but getting closer hampers rather than improves the view. The Hanson Lakes region is managed as trailless, although hikers have beaten a primitive route ascending well north of the falls.

View from Observation Peak

18 OBSERVATION PEAK

Best for: hiking
16.6 miles round trip
Strenuous
Elevation gain: 2,614 feet
High point: 9,151 feet
Hikable: mid-July through October
Map: USGS Stanley Lake

After an all-day trek to Observation Peak (9,151 feet), you'll revel in a sprawling Sawtooth panorama of the likes usually seen only by climbers or pilots. Use directions in trip 16 to reach Stanley Lake and trip 17 for the 3.4 miles to Bridal Veil Falls viewpoint. Continue up Stanley Lake Creek along the old Greenback Mine Road, passing at 6.2 miles a road to the abandoned mine.

After another 0.8 mile, reach a three-way junction. Observation Peak is 1.3 miles and 1,119 feet above to the west (right); the trail to McGown Lakes, Sawtooth and Alpine lakes, and Iron Creek trailhead goes east (trip 15).

The hike ends splendidly atop bare Observation Peak, 8.3 miles and a 2,614-foot increase in elevation from Stanley Lake. To help identify peaks (Warbonnet, Tohobit, Big Baron Spire, Mount Regan, and Cony Peak among them), bring a compass and the Sawtooth Wilderness contour map (scale 1:48,000) sold at ranger stations.

If you are an ambitious day hiker, leave from Stanley Lake at daybreak to reach Observation Peak for lunch and views, then venture on to McGown Lakes–Sawtooth Lake–Iron Creek trailhead to a shuttled car. It's a 17.3-mile strenuous trip.

Redfish Lake

SAWTOOTH NATIONAL FOREST
Sawtooth National Recreation Area

19 REDFISH LAKE WALKS

Best for: short walks
Opportunities for: biking
0.1 mile to 1.2 miles round trip
Easy
Elevation gain: negligible
High point: 6,760 feet
Hikable: mid-May through October
Map: USGS Stanley

Redfish Lake is named for the sockeye salmon, a magnificent scarlet fish that was once plentiful in Sawtooth Country. Now only a dozen or fewer of the red salmon return from the Pacific Ocean to spawn in Redfish Lake. The lake has endured the twentieth century far better than the sockeye. Redfish Lake, 1,502 acres, is the reigning "people's choice" of Sawtooth Country, much loved and much visited. In summer its campgrounds are in constant demand. White beaches lure families with their sandbuckets to mingle with sailboaters, windsurfers, and water skiers.

To reach Redfish Lake from Stanley, drive south for 4.3 miles and turn right on paved Redfish Lake Road 214, leading 2.2 miles to Redfish Lake Lodge. From Ketchum, drive 57.5 miles north on Highway 75 to the same turnoff. Even the access road offers a visual surprise as it climbs gently toward the lake: a long look at Mount Heyburn, whose tangle of granite spires is a sort of Sawtooth Statue of Liberty welcoming weary lowlanders to the uplifting, revitalizing high country.

Old bear trap along Bench Lakes trail

Fishhook Creek Nature Trail
0.4 mile round trip

Walk east from Redfish Lake Lodge above the lakeshore on paved road for a few hundred yards (this part is closed to motorized travel), and take a path uphill to the Redfish Visitor Center and the beginning of the Fishhook Nature Trail. You can also drive to the Visitor Center on a fork of road 214. The interpretive-signed nature path goes a brief, but educational, 200 yards through beaver ponds and bird habitat. One sign explains that the wooded northwest ridge above the lake, which partially blocks the view of Mount Heyburn, is a lateral moraine, several hundred feet high, left by a glacier that geologists estimate was 1,000 feet thick. A terminal moraine forms the end (or dam) of Redfish Lake. The last major glaciers were recent in geological terms, occurring 10,000 years ago.

If you visit Fishhook Creek from July to October, look for trout-sized, red kokanee (landlocked) salmon that spawn in shallow, graveled sections of the stream.

Wooden Bear Trap
1.2 miles round trip

This log antique is left from a time when settlers and sheepmen wanted to curb the large numbers of grizzlies and black bears (grizzlies were totally eliminated in Sawtooth land). To see the log trap, walk or bike from Redfish Lodge north (back toward Highway 75) on the paved access road until it crosses Fishhook Creek at 0.2 mile. Look left for a trail sign. Redfish Lake trailhead is on the right. Take the Bench Lakes–Marshall Lakes trail, on the left, which begins as a bouldery, washed-out jeep road.

Within a few minutes of uphill walking, at 0.6 mile from the lodge, start looking for a footbridge over the stream. Cross the bridge to a shaded flat and the low, strong, log trap. Similar wooden structures, less intact, are scattered throughout the Sawtooth foothills, their hidden locations known to old-timers. As you return toward road 214, go the last few hundred yards on a more interesting, primitive trail through woods near Fishhook Creek.

Little Redfish Lake
0.2 mile round trip

You can drive or bike to Little Redfish shoreline, but most travelers hurry past as they head for Redfish Lake. Yet, photographers prize the chance to capture the cluster of Mount Heyburn, Horstman Peak, and Mount Ebert (and perhaps Thompson Peak and Williams Peak—the pair farther north) reflected on Little Redfish. The shimmering waters are motor-free, making the lake's two campgrounds favorites for canoers and rowboat fishermen. To see Little Redfish Lake, drive or bike from Redfish Lake Lodge 1.7 miles to Mountain View Campground or 1.8 miles to nearby Chinook Bay Campground (if biking, the return trip is noticeably uphill). Avoid parking in designated pay campsites as you leave for your lakeside photo stroll.

Redfish Lake Rock Shelter
0.1 mile round trip

The Rock Shelter is just north of Little Redfish Lake 0.3 mile. From Redfish Lake Lodge, drive or bicycle down the access road 2.1 miles (almost to Highway 75). Just past Little Redfish Lake, look for the visitor information pullout—and picnic-plate message center (you can't miss the white plates and their scrawled messages). A bridge crosses Redfish Lake Creek and leads directly to the overhang, which was used by prehistoric hunters, and later, by Sheepeater Indians.

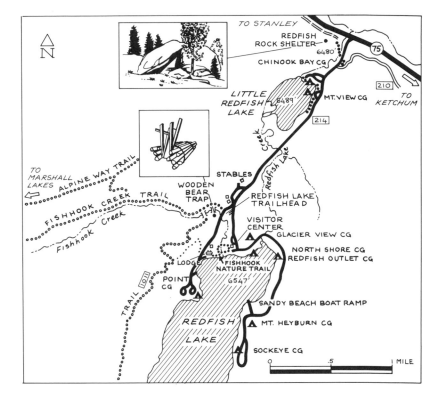

20 REDFISH TRAILHEAD
CLASSIC HIKE I: *BENCH LAKES*

Best for: hiking
7 miles round trip
Moderate
Elevation gain: 1,290 feet (and loss)
High point: 7,480 feet
Hikable: mid-June through October
Maps: USGS Stanley, Mount Cramer

Ask a local to recommend a short hike near Redfish Lake and the likely reply will be "Bench Lakes." The easy answer stems from the route's modest distance, the manageable 1,290-foot elevation gain, and, most of all, a ridge-top panorama of 4-mile-long, shimmering Redfish Lake. The unpretentious Bench Lakes are much visited because of their closeness to Redfish campgrounds. June is the best month for a trip; in July and August the Bench Lakes route is a dusty trek with many horses and hikers going your way.

Although families frequently go to Bench Lakes, there are easier, more interesting Redfish area trips for children, including Fishhook Creek Meadow (trip 21), Lily Lake (trip 22), and Grand Mogul trail (trip 23). Follow directions in trip 19 to reach Redfish Lake. The first section of Bench Lakes trail has been rerouted since the 1963 Stanley topo; it now begins near Redfish Lake trailhead 0.3 mile north of Redfish Lake Lodge. The trailhead is sometimes difficult for newcomers to find. If coming from Highway 75 up the Redfish Lake road, drive 1.7 miles, bypass the lodge turnoff, and go 50 yards farther to the signed trailhead parking lot entrance.

At the trailhead, cross the pavement and head up a rocky old roadbed which is Redfish Lake Creek Trail 102, but usually called the Bench Lakes trail, at least until it reaches Redfish Lake Creek in Redfish canyon 5 miles away.

Go 0.3 mile to a signed T intersection and turn left, crossing Fishhook Creek by bridge (this is the last water until the first Bench Lake). The worn path climbs through dry, lodgepole pine forest, past a registration box, and gradually reaches the ridge. At 3 miles, by large granite boulders, a highpoint overlooks Redfish Lake.

Next the trail forks: right goes 0.5 mile to the first Bench Lake, straight goes 2 miles down to Inlet Campground at the end of Redfish Lake. Caution: many weary, gazing hikers intending to see Bench Lakes have missed this turnoff. The Bench Lakes route drops briefly off the ridge to a swale and then climbs a burned slope before reaching the first shallow woodland lake. The next lake, much larger, is a few hundred yards away. The maintained trail ends, but cross-country travelers can advance onward to the higher lakes pressed against Mount Heyburn. Since guided trailrides and many hikers visit the first two Bench Lakes, try to avoid camping there.

Fishhook Creek Meadows and Horstmann Peak (left), Mount Ebert (center), and east shoulder of Thompson Peak (right)

Alternative Hike: Bench Lakes Trail One Way

    Redfish Lake trailhead to Inlet Transfer Camp
      (requires shuttle boat)
    5 miles
    Moderate
    Elevation gain: 922 feet; loss 920 feet

Another Bench Lakes trip takes advantage of shuttle boat service from Redfish Lake Lodge to the Inlet Campground boatdock (see note below). Follow directions above for the first 3 miles to the Bench Lakes turnoff. Stay left (unless a side trip is planned to Bench Lakes), descending the ridge for 1.4 miles to another junction, where a side trail goes 0.6 mile to Inlet Campground.

This distance can be walked either way, but the north-to-south (lodge-to-inlet) route described here has two advantages: the elevation gain of about 920 feet (from either starting point) is spread over 3 miles rather than 2 miles. Also, Redfish Lake and Sawtooth scenery are saved for last. When hiking from inlet to the lodge, watch for trail intersections, particularly the easy-to-miss turnoff to Bench Lakes. And bring water, more than usual—the hardy climb from Redfish Inlet is in full sun.

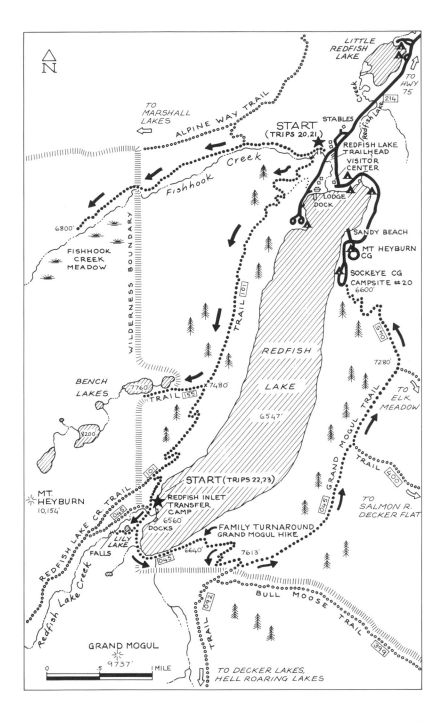

LITTLE REDFISH LAKE

TO HWY 75

Redfish Lake 214

TO MARSHALL LAKES

ALPINE WAY TRAIL

START (TRIPS 20,21)

STABLES

REDFISH LAKE TRAILHEAD

VISITOR CENTER

Fishhook Creek

LODGE DOCK

SANDY BEACH

MT HEYBURN CG

SOCKEYE CG
CAMPSITE #20
6600'

6800'

FISHHOOK CREEK MEADOW

WILDERNESS BOUNDARY

TRAIL 101

REDFISH LAKE
6547'

7280'

TRAIL 540

TO ELK MEADOW

BENCH LAKES

7760'

TRAIL 155

X 7480'

8200'

GRAND MOGUL TRAIL 045

TRAIL 400

TO SALMON R. DECKER FLAT

MT. HEYBURN
10,154'

REDFISH LAKE CR. TRAIL

101

045

START (TRIPS 22,23)

REDFISH INLET TRANSFER CAMP
6560'

DOCKS

LILY LAKE

FALLS

045

FAMILY TURNAROUND
GRAND MOGUL HIKE

6640'

7613'

TRAIL 092

BULL MOOSE TRAIL

TRAIL 399

Redfish Lake Creek

GRAND MOGUL
9737'

0   .5   1 MILE

TO DECKER LAKES,
HELL ROARING LAKES

N

SHUTTLE BOAT: Arrange at Redfish Lake Lodge boatdock for a pickup time at Inlet Campground boatdock. In midseason the afternoon pickups are usually at 4, 6, and 8 P.M., or by appointment. Play it safe and confirm a time. Departures from the lodge to the inlet are by demand. Cost in 1989 was $4 per person one way, or $7 round trip.

SAWTOOTH NATIONAL FOREST
Sawtooth National Recreation Area

21 REDFISH TRAILHEAD CLASSIC HIKE II: *FISHHOOK CREEK MEADOW*

Best for: hiking
4.4 miles round trip
Easy
Elevation gain: 250 feet
High point: 6,800 feet
Hikable: June through October
Map: USGS Stanley

Wading among the lilies at Lily Lake

Fishhook Creek flows *into* Redfish Lake, and Redfish Lake Creek flows *out* a scant half mile to the east. Sometimes the two streams are mistaken, one for the other. Many other hikes in this book follow Redfish Lake Creek trail at the far end of Redfish Lake. This trip goes up Fishhook Creek to Fishhook Creek Meadow, just over 2 miles from Redfish Lake. The gentle 2.2-mile path to the meadows is easy enough for children.

Mileage begins at Redfish Lake trailhead, 0.3 mile north of Redfish Lake Lodge. See trip 20, Bench Lakes, for help in locating the trailhead. Follow the Bench Lakes trail, which starts as a rocky road for 0.4 mile until it crosses Fishhook Creek. Don't cross. Stay right, along the stream, and at 0.8 mile, pass the turnoff for Alpine Way trail to Marshall Lakes. The nearly level Fishhook Creek trail saunters along, and at 1 mile a side path detours to the creek and a child-beckoning footbridge. Explore. A few yards farther up the trail is the registration box.

At 1.3 miles, the road becomes a narrow trail and strays from the clear, lazy stream. You might spot mule deer and perhaps a roving skunk. Expect mosquitoes in June and July and bring repellent. The path undulates until reaching the wilderness boundary and Fishhook Creek Meadow at 2.2 miles. Horstman Peak is the imposing giant to the left of the Fishhook drainage; Mount Ebert is centered above the distant upper canyon. Past the meadow the path eventually becomes lost in washouts and deadfall.

Presently, mountain bikers are using the Fishhook Creek trail, but the Forest Service is not advocating wheeled use, and abuse will bring a closure. If you do ride to the meadow, avoid going early in the season when the path is muddy. Be extra courteous to walkers.

Redfish Lake Inlet

SAWTOOTH NATIONAL FOREST
Sawtooth National Recreation Area

22 LILY LAKE, REDFISH LAKE CREEK FALLS

Best for: hiking
1 mile round trip from Redfish Inlet (use shuttle boat)
Easy
Elevation gain: 160 feet
High point: 6,720 feet
Hikable: June through October
Map: USGS Mount Cramer

A swift boat ride across 4-mile-long Redfish Lake leads to the Redfish Inlet Transfer Camp where some of the most demanding hikes and climbs in the Sawtooth Wilderness depart. But from this same trailhead, a short walk leads to teacup-sized Lily Lake which offers up frogs and lily pads.

Follow directions to Redfish Lake (trip 19) and check with the lodge for shuttle boat departure times and cost (see shuttle explanation in trip 20, Bench Lakes). If you're hesitant about spending money in order to go hiking, just remember all the dusty miles you've walked for free. And the boat ride to the wilderness frontier is fun—kids will be gung-ho for a Lily Lake escapade (or the short outing to follow: trip 23, Grand Mogul).

The boat drops passengers at Redfish Inlet, which has picnic tables, campsites, two docks, and on calm-water days, numerous water skiers. Walk through the picnic area to the new footbridge placed over churning Redfish Lake Creek in fall 1988. The bridge installation ended an era of daring crossings on a sturdy log a few hundred yards upstream. (You might rather walk the log. Your kids will.)

Lily Lake is a scant 0.5 mile away on a signed path and 160 feet higher than the inlet. You may see spruce grouse crouching along the trail or in branches overhead.

At Lily Lake, flat slabs of sparkling granite beckon to a rest in the Sawtooth sun. Youngsters will want to wade and walk the logs along the shallow shore. Ask them to leave the lilies intact.

To see a falls on Redfish Lake Creek and views up Redfish canyon, walk around the pond to the left (south) and up a short trail to the steep bank above the stream. Supervise children closely. Allow about 2 hours for a Lily Lake adventure. For a longer family outing, combine Lily Lake with trip 23, Grand Mogul.

(Redfish Inlet is also reached by the 5-mile-long Bench Lakes–Redfish Lake Creek trail from Redfish Lake trailhead—see trip 20. A popular choice is to hike one way and boat the other.)

SAWTOOTH NATIONAL FOREST
Sawtooth National Recreation Area

23 GRAND MOGUL TRAIL

Best for: hiking
2 miles round trip from Redfish Inlet (use shuttle boat)
Easy
Elevation gain: negligible
High point: 6,640 feet
Hikable: mid-June through October
Map: USGS Mount Cramer

Grand Mogul (9,733 feet) rises above the southern tip of Redfish Lake, a grandiose mountain, although less recognized than its neighbor across Redfish canyon, Mount Heyburn (10,154 feet). Both are widely photographed and admired by Redfish Lake visitors. A Grand Mogul outing can be a brief and relaxing 2 miles or a more strenuous hike the length of Redfish ridge 6.5 miles back to Sockeye Campground.

Resting after a Grand Mogul adventure (boat dock at Redfish Lake Inlet, Grand Mogul in distance)

Redfish Lake from Grand Mogul trail

Take the shuttle boat from Redfish Lake Lodge dock to the Redfish Inlet Transfer Camp at the lake's far end (see trip 20, Bench Lakes, and trip 22, Lily Lake, for shuttle information). Cross the new footbridge and follow signs toward Lily Lake, strolling through thick, aromatic woods.

Stay left at 0.3 mile when the trail forks uphill to Lily Lake (0.2 mile away). Grand Mogul trail hugs the steep shoreline of Redfish Lake for the next few hundred yards, crossing rocks and small gullies.

The trail then passes beneath the sun-blocking hulk of Grand Mogul, crossing a rivulet from a tiny lake 0.5 mile farther and 480 feet higher. Move through a forest canopy reminiscent of the damp Cascades.

When the fir needle–cushioned path starts to climb steadily, you've come a long mile from Redfish Inlet and reached the family-hike turnaround. The trail continues another 5.5 miles, ending at Sockeye Campground.

Alternative Hike: Grand Mogul Trail from Redfish Inlet to Sockeye Campground

> 6.5 miles one way (use shuttle boat)
> Moderate
> Elevation gain: 1,043 feet; loss 900 feet
> High point: 7,613 feet
> Maps: USGS Stanley, Mount Cramer

Follow directions above and climb vigorously from the lake for a long mile on switchbacks, gaining 1,013 feet elevation, with lake views and Cabin Creek Peak seen to the far north. There may be deadfall here since Grand Mogul and other trails in this vicinity have low maintenance priority.

At the ridge, go north (left) along the dry, lodgepole-covered moraine for 2.8 miles. (The route heading south winds 10 miles through timber to Hell Roaring Lake.) The trees provide shade but allow only glimpses of Redfish and the 'tooths. The final 1.5 miles drops quickly, losing 680 feet of elevation by trail's end at 6.5 miles—Sockeye Campground 1.5 miles from Redfish Lake Lodge. Either walk to the lodge where your trip began or meet a shuttle car (or locked bicycle) left at Sockeye Campground.

If taking this hike in reverse (clockwise), look for the trail's start near camp-site number 20. (More signs and trailhead improvements are planned.) The elevation gain of 900 feet is more gradual going clockwise and the superb scenery is saved for last. Arrange for a boat ride back or walk the 5-mile Bench Lakes trail for a round-the-lake loop (bring plenty of water).

SAWTOOTH NATIONAL FOREST
Sawtooth Wilderness

24 GARDEN OF GIANTS, FLAT ROCK JUNCTION

Best for: hiking
7 miles round trip from Redfish Inlet (use shuttle boat)
Moderate
Elevation gain: 800 feet
High point: 7,400 feet
Hikable: July through October
Maps: USGS Mount Cramer, Warbonnet Peak

Turnaround at Garden of Giants

3.2 miles round trip
Moderate
Elevation gain: 640 feet
High point: 7,200 feet
Hikable: mid-June through October

These two destinations offer a chance for families to experience Redfish Lake Creek canyon, the wilderness land seen from the shores of Redfish Lake. Garden of Giants is a granite encampment of boxcar-sized boulders in Redfish can-yon. Farther on, at Flat Rock Junction, the granite is pancake flat. Go to Gar-den of Giants anytime after the snow leaves, but not until August is Redfish Lake Creek low enough to expose the smooth, polished streambed that gave Flat Rock Junction its name.

For hikers the easiest access to Redfish canyon is by shuttle boat across Redfish Lake (see trip 20, Bench Lakes for shuttle information). From Redfish

Inlet Transfer Camp, walk through the picnic area, uphill to the pole fence and registration box where trail 045 begins. It connects to Redfish Lake Creek Trail 101 in 0.8 mile, gaining a significant 440 feet elevation. Take it slow—this is the toughest stretch of the trip. At the T intersection, go left. Your route follows signs pointing toward Cramer Lakes and Baron Lakes.

Travel up Redfish canyon through rockfall that's tumbled from Mount Heyburn's southeast crags. Look ahead to the southwest to see the unmistakable Saddleback Peak (trip 25). Gain an effortless 200 feet elevation in the next 0.8 mile to Garden of Giants. Once, an old, white-lettered sign served a greeting, but it's gone.

You've arrived when you see a merry-go-round-sized boulder resting on its edges with a yard-high crawl space underneath. Here hikers have waited out storms and trusting campers have slept. After you, too, cautiously hunker under the mammoth rock, go out and climb and wander in the granite carnival beneath Mount Heyburn.

Nearly 2 miles farther up the trail is Flat Rock Junction. On the way, 0.8 mile past Garden of Giants, is more granite, but in the form of large slabs above the rushing stream. The slabs mark the turnoff for Saddleback Peak, Elephant's Perch, and Saddleback Lakes. The trail toward Flat Rock Junction

This old sign has disappeared

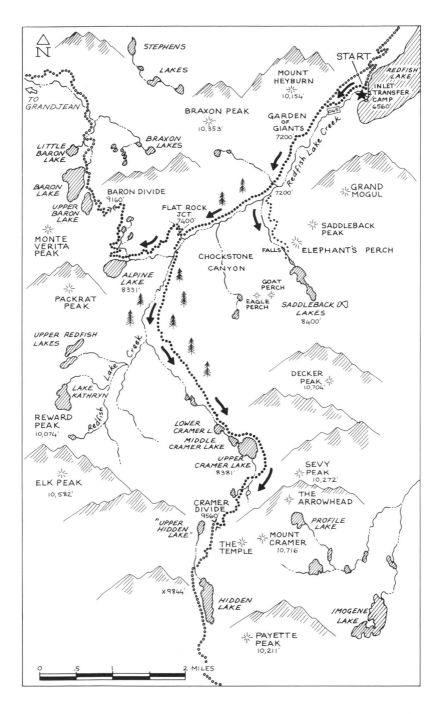

N

STEPHENS
LAKES

TO
GRANDJEAN

MOUNT
HEYBURN
10,154'

START

REDFISH
LAKE

INLET
TRANSFER
CAMP
6560'

BRAXON PEAK
10,353'

GARDEN
OF
GIANTS
7200'

045

Redfish Lake Creek

LITTLE
BARON
LAKE

BRAXON
LAKES

GRAND
MOGUL

BARON
LAKE

BARON DIVIDE
9160'

7200'

UPPER
BARON
LAKE

FLAT ROCK
JCT.
7400'

SADDLEBACK
PEAK

MONTE
VERITA
PEAK

CHOCKSTONE
CANYON

FALLS

ELEPHANT'S PERCH

ALPINE
LAKE
8331'

GOAT
PERCH

PACKRAT
PEAK

EAGLE
PERCH

SADDLEBACK
LAKES
8400'

UPPER REDFISH
LAKES

Redfish Lake Creek

DECKER
PEAK
10,704'

LAKE
KATHRYN

REWARD
PEAK
10,074'

LOWER
CRAMER L.
MIDDLE
CRAMER LAKE
UPPER
CRAMER LAKE
8381'

SEVY
PEAK
10,272'

ELK PEAK
10,582'

THE
ARROWHEAD

CRAMER
DIVIDE
9560'

"UPPER
HIDDEN
LAKE"

PROFILE
LAKE

THE
TEMPLE

MOUNT
CRAMER
10,716'

x 9844'

HIDDEN
LAKE

IMOGENE
LAKE

PAYETTE
PEAK
10,211'

0   .5   1   2 MILES

ascends gradually, deeper into higher mountains. At 3.2 miles, look southwest for Chockstone Peak where a giant chockstone is wedged between two spires.

Arrive in 3.5 miles at Flat Rock Junction, where the trail divides: right goes to Alpine Lake and Baron Divide (trip 26); left to Cramer Lakes (trip 27). Between these trails a narrow path winds to the stream. Follow it to find the sheets of water-worn granite stretching bank to bank in Redfish Lake Creek. Early in the season an unwadable torrent hides the flat rock. By August, shallow flows let weary hikers sit or lay upon the streambed—a chilling Sawtooth ritual. Nearby are plentiful private tent sites where backpackers can set up base camp for day trips deeper into the wilderness. When you leave the high country, watch closely for the cutoff trail 045 to the lake and shuttle boat.

SAWTOOTH NATIONAL FOREST
Sawtooth Wilderness

25 ELEPHANT'S PERCH, SADDLEBACK LAKES

Best for: hiking
7.6 miles round trip from Redfish Inlet (use shuttle boat)
Difficult
Elevation gain: 1,840 feet
High point: 8,400 feet
Hikable: mid-July through September
Map: USGS Mount Cramer

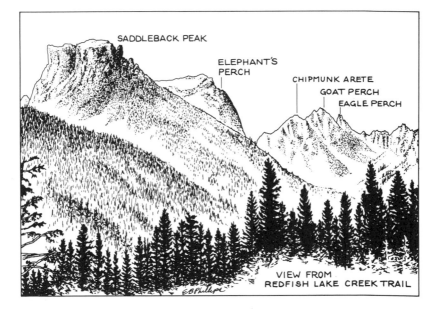

The Elephant's Perch towers over the largest Saddleback Lake.

Saddleback Peak is the unofficial name given to a broad, saddle-shaped granite mountain rising above Redfish canyon. The peak's west face is a popular climbing wall called the Elephant's Perch. Two other jutting points across Saddleback Lake basin are known as Goat Perch and Eagle Perch. A nickname is given to the Saddleback Lake vicinity, one that applies to many Sawtooth hideaways: Shangri-la. A primitive trail from Redfish canyon to the first Saddleback Lake can be followed by seasoned hikers comfortable in route finding. Bring a topo map.

Take the shuttle boat from Redfish Lake dock to Redfish Inlet Transfer Camp (see trip 20, Bench Lakes for shuttle information). Follow directions in trip 24 (Flat Rock Junction) up Redfish canyon for 2.3 miles to the granite slabs above Redfish Lake Creek that mark the turnoff to Saddleback canyon. Walk on the granite, upstream, and find a path leading through brush to a crossing on logs and boulders—impassable in high water.

Cross the stream and look for a shrubby path on the south shore which ascends, fading in and out, through woods, over and around rock benches. Avoid the outlet ravine to the west of Saddleback canyon. Your destination is toward the western base of Saddleback Peak. The last steep pitch gains 400 feet elevation on loose dirt and rock, with handholds on stunted alpine firs. Nearby, over your right shoulder, the lake's outlet stream plummets down a rockface in a section known as The Waterfall.

When you reach the security of the first crevice of a lake, cross to its western, bouldery shoreline and crane your neck to search for climbers on the wall of the Elephant's Perch. For a wide-angle photo of the Yosemite-type wall, go to the larger, second lake and circle to the southwest shore. Explore further in Shangri-La—a third lake is nearby.

SAWTOOTH NATIONAL FOREST
Sawtooth Wilderness

26 ALPINE LAKE, BARON DIVIDE

Best for: hiking
13 miles round trip from Redfish Inlet (use shuttle boat)
Strenuous
Elevation gain: 2,600 feet
High point: 9,160 feet
Hikable: mid-July through September
Maps: USGS Mount Cramer, Warbonnet Peak

Turnaround at Alpine Lake
10 miles round trip
Moderate
Elevation gain: 1,800 feet
High point: 8,360 feet

Alpine Lake is the closest large lake reachable by trail in the Redfish area. A steady stream of plucky hikers, many on their first overnight backcountry trip, enliven its scenic shoreline throughout the summer. Above Alpine Lake the trail winds to Baron Divide, a destination synonymous with wilderness. The divide overlooks Baron Lakes in wild Baron Creek canyon. Most travelers go no farther than Alpine Lake. Yet, with an early start (take the first shuttle boat across Redfish after breakfast) you can be at Baron Divide by noon.

The trip begins with a ride across Redfish Lake on the shuttle boat. (See trip 20, Bench Lakes, for shuttle information.) Take the Redfish Lake Creek canyon trail for 3.5 miles to Flat Rock Junction (trip 24). Go right on the Alpine Lake, Baron Divide Trail 101. From Flat Rock Junction, climb up long, sunny switchbacks, past pastel patches of pink spirea, and steadily gain broader views of Redfish and Cramer canyons. At 5 miles (the 1.5 miles from Flat Rock Junction feels longer than it is), arrive at Alpine Lake, aptly named. Campfires are prohibited, to protect the struggling alpine conifers.

Another 1.5 miles, and 720 feet higher, is Baron Divide. Walk there on worn trail, passing three small lakes and flowery parklands. Your goal, Baron Divide, is on the west-northwest skyline. Snowdrifts may block this trail section until late July or longer.

Baron Lakes and "Old Smoothie" (Big Baron Spire) from Baron Divide

From the divide, maneuver among storm-torn whitebark pines to look upon exquisite Baron Lakes. To the west is Big Baron Spire (also called "Old Smoothie"), resembling a jutting giant thumb. The southwest skyline is the multipinnacled Verita Ridge (also Monte Verita).

Use willpower to resist the tempting descent to Upper Baron Lake and the land bridge separating it from Baron Lake—you've a boat to meet 6.5 miles away at Redfish Inlet. Watch the time. If you sleep in or overstay your divide visit, prepare to join the lug-soled legions who have fled the sunny and often-rocky trail back to Inlet dock to catch the 6 P.M. or 8 P.M. boat (covering the distance in less than 2 hours is admirable).

SAWTOOTH NATIONAL FOREST
Sawtooth Wilderness

27 CRAMER LAKES, THE TEMPLE, CRAMER DIVIDE

Best for: hiking
Strenuous
18.6 miles round trip from Redfish Inlet (use shuttle boat)
Elevation gain: 3,160 feet
High point: 9,560 feet
Hikable: late July through mid-September
Maps: USGS Mount Cramer, Warbonnet Peak

Turnaround at Upper Cramer Lake Inlet
14.0 miles round trip
Moderate to strenuous
Elevation gain: 2,000 feet
High point: 8,400 feet

Three landmarks in Cramer Lakes canyon are commonly photographed: the waterfall at Middle Cramer Lake and two rock formations, The Arrowhead and The Temple. Of these three, the last is an ambitious goal for a day hike. Middle Cramer Lake is 7 miles from Redfish Lake Inlet, and a first view of The Temple is a long mile farther. Once there, it's hard to resist going for Cramer Divide at 9.3 miles before turning back. A day trip just to Cramer Lakes is fairly strenuous. Getting to the divide is downright hard work.

Take an early boat from Redfish Lake dock to Redfish Inlet, or for the most hours afield, plan to camp overnight at the inlet (see trip 20, Bench Lakes, for shuttle information). Go 3.5 miles to Flat Rock Junction (trip 24). Turn left at Flatrock Junction and search for the driest crossing of Redfish Lake Creek—on a logjam downstream from the horse ford or upstream across granite slabs. In high runoff (June into July), all choices may be dangerous and impassable. Check with the Forest Service for conditions. If turned back, do as others have done and go instead to Alpine Lake and Baron Divide (trip 26).

After the crossing, hike for 3 miles through shady timber, paying your dues

The Temple

for the alpine glitter waiting at Cramer Lakes and beyond. The elevation gain is a moderate 1,120 feet from Flat Rock Junction to Lower Cramer Lake at 6.5 miles.

Lower Cramer Lake is green and placid. In a few more minutes, at 6.7 miles, you're at Middle Cramer and its much-admired waterfall that pours in from Upper Cramer Lake. A prized campsite (there are no poor ones here) is adjacent to the thundering falls. On the eastern skyline the Sawtooth's largest arrowhead points skyward. A short walk reaches the large upper lake, and its inlet park of cushioned grass is at 7 miles. South of The Arrowhead rises Mount Cramer (10,716 feet). If you're weary, stop here and linger in the Cramer parkland before heading home. You'll have no rest in the over 2-mile upward climb toward The Temple and Cramer Divide, a gain of 1,160 feet. If thunderstorms threaten, forego the shelterless ascent to the divide.

Leaving Upper Cramer, the trail climbs a notch and rises 400 feet in a mile to reach a shallow pond set in scree. The pond mirrors The Temple's towers. To go farther is to enter a stark, rough-and-tumble realm where the path has been forced through boulders and scree, with repeated switchbacks, gaining 660 feet more to reach the pass at 9.3 miles. (Total elevation gain from Redfish Inlet is 3,160 feet).

From the windswept divide, all views are southward. The vast country ahead drains the South Fork Payette River. A silver sliver of lake ("Upper Hidden") lies west in the bare ravine below the trail. Hidden Lake, a deep wilderness gem, is still hidden 1.4 miles and 900 feet below to the south. A few hikers have made it there and back in a day—very few. As you tarry on the divide, remember the long miles back to meet the shuttle boat.

Hell Roaring

SAWTOOTH NATIONAL FOREST
Sawtooth National Recreation Area

28 HELL ROARING CREEK POND

Best for: hiking
Easy
3.2 miles round trip
Elevation gain: 360 feet
High point: 7,160 feet
Hikable: mid-May through October
Map: USGS Obsidian

This outing is a tame 3.2-mile walk, excellent for children, along Hell Roaring Creek to a fameless, nameless, woodland pond (not to be mistaken for the glamorous alpine visit to Hell Roaring Lake, trip 29). All seasons are good ones for this brief journey. Early summer snowmelt brings thundering water, while July brings flowers (and bugs). August dries the Hell Roaring swamplands. Autumn turns them bronze. An evening walk will likely bring sightings of deer, maybe elk.

Reach the lower Hell Roaring trailhead by going 46.9 miles from Ketchum north on Highway 75. From Stanley, go south on Highway 75 for 15 miles. Look for a sign reading "Decker Flat, Fourth of July Road." Turn west on Decker Flat Road 210, cross the Salmon River and turn left, upstream, on Hell Roaring Road 315; it's 0.4 mile to the trail. A new trailhead is also scheduled to be built in 1990 near where the road crosses Hell Roaring Creek. Once it's built, expect heavy use by horses and packstock.

The path begins in sage, climbs for 0.2 mile, and briefly overlooks the stream. Next it turns north in lodgepole forest, brightened in June with heart-leaf arnica, phlox, and Indian paint brush. Wind through rock outcroppings where hefty muscles pried hefty boulders aside. At 0.3 mile, the path again traverses above Hell Roaring Creek. Views south show the Sawtooth Valley, east are the White Cloud foothills. To the southwest three summits stand out: McDonald Peak, Parks Peak, and Imogene Peak. These landmarks tower over Alice Lake and Toxaway Lake canyons. (Also recognizable to hikers familiar with Alice Lake is the granite monolith, El Capitan.)

At 0.6 mile, the roar vanishes and Hell Roaring Creek becomes a silent, translucent stream. Now children can wander safely, though through soggy grass, to water's edge. The woodland is thick with snowberry, blooming in early summer with tiny white and pink bell-shaped blossoms. This section of trail is directly across from the Hell Roaring Lake access road.

After 0.8 mile and a modest 300 feet elevation gain from the Salmon River,

Killdeer eggs

the new trail meets the old trail. At 1.3 miles, just past a muddy stretch, start watching closely for a dry riverbed going right (north). Follow the black and tan boulders a few hundred yards to the shallow, rock-lined pond Walk around the shore and look west. In the far distance is the granite skyline that rises over Hell Roaring Lake, including The Arrowhead.

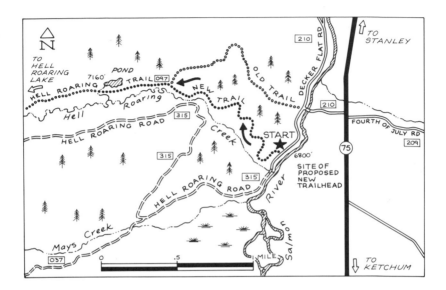

SAWTOOTH NATIONAL FOREST
Sawtooth Wilderness

29 HELL ROARING LAKE, FINGER OF FATE

Best for: hiking
3.6 miles round trip
Easy
Elevation gain: 200 feet
High point: 7,400 feet
Hikable: mid-June to October
Maps: USGS Mount Cramer, Snowyside Peak

Hell Roaring and Fourth of July lakes (see trip 50 for the latter) have long provided parents and children their first overnight family wilderness experi-

Crossing boulders to reach Hell Roaring Creek Pond

ence. Both lakes are reached by a short, nearly level 1.8-mile cakewalk with more extreme hiking nearby. Until 1992 when the Fourth of July Road was reconstructed, both lakes had histories of notorious access roads. The Hell Roaring Road still requires a high-clearance vehicle (four-wheel drive is helpful), boulder dodging, and patience. The SNRA is considering closing the road to the upper Hell Roaring trailhead in the future. (Owners of low-clearance cars, see note below.)

To reach Hell Roaring Lake, follow directions in trip 28 to lower Hell Roaring trailhead by the Salmon River. Cross Hell Roaring Creek and drive on road 315 another 4.4 miles (about 45 minutes) to upper Hell Roaring trailhead. The worst road section comes in the steep second mile, directly after the Y inter-section with Mays Creek, when Hell Roaring Road bends right and climbs sharply. Clear the first ditch and you'll manage the rest. Four-wheel-drive passenger cars can handle it. The next slanted, hillside mile has limited pullouts. Once on top, the forested moraine is fraught with cobbles, but level, for 2.5 miles to road's end.

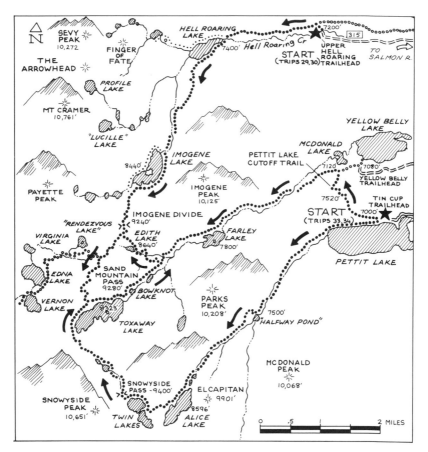

At the upper trailhead, balance across a subdued Hell Roaring Creek on narrow logs and reach the registration box at the wilderness boundary. Hell Roaring Lake is 1.8 miles away but unseen until the trail arrives at the wooded shore. From the outlet bridge, look across to the granite amphitheater filling the western horizon. Standing out—the Finger of Fate spire. To its left on the skyline is the miniature silhouette of The Arrowhead. Both landmarks are visible from Highway 75 in the Sawtooth Valley. The trailless canyon to the southwest holds Profile Lake.

For a longer hike of 1 to 2 miles, stay on the main trail toward Imogene Lake (trip 30). Climb the switchbacks out of Hell Roaring Lake high enough for an overlook of the lake and spectacular granite scenery to the west. For scramblers, there's another choice—an arduous trek in the stone playground adjacent to Finger of Fate and upper lakes. A path leaves Hell Roaring for the first upper lake. Find it by taking the primitive foot trail around the lake's west side to a campsite just before the sizeable outlet stream from upper Hell Roaring Lakes. Don't cross the stream, but look for an overgrown trail going straight uphill from the campsite through thick timber. After struggling 0.8 mile and gaining 800 feet elevation, arrive at the first and largest upper lake—a springboard for higher alpine adventures. If you're an experienced hiker, weave upward through a gully and boulder maze, along granite boulevards, tiptoeing through velvety moss gardens.

(For low-clearance car owners: To avoid the access road, start from the Salmon River at the lower Hell Roaring trailhead, a 5-mile hike. Stay on the main path to the lake. Horsemen use this route, but it's a long plod for hikers, especially for kids.)

SAWTOOTH NATIONAL FOREST
Sawtooth Wilderness

30 IMOGENE LAKE, IMOGENE DIVIDE

Best for: hiking
11.8 miles round trip
Moderate
Elevation gain: 1,240 feet
High point: 8,440 feet
Hikable: July through September
Maps: USGS Mount Cramer, Snowyside Peak

Imogene Lake resembles another Sawtooth Wilderness gem, Toxaway Lake (trip 34). Each is reached by a hike of about 6 miles and a mild elevation gain of almost 1,200 feet. Both have irregular shorelines and scattered fairyland-like islands. From Imogene or Toxaway, a week of alpine sightseeing is at hand. The only glitch—the infamous access roads. Hell Roaring Road is described in trip 29.

Imogene Lake is a natural extension beyond the easy 1.8-mile hike to Hell

Imogene Lake from Imogene Divide

Roaring Lake. From Hell Roaring inlet bridge, it's another 4.1 miles, and a casual 1,000-foot rise, to Imogene. Leave before breakfast to see Imogene on a day hike—partly because of the rough, slow road, but also because, besides Imogene, there are another dozen lakes and tarns nearby to explore, plus ridges and divides to climb. For conditioned hikers an Imogene day hike is tiring, but not overwhelming. However, families with young children should consider making Imogene an overnight trip.

Follow directions in trip 29 to Hell Roaring Lake and cross the inlet bridge, going south along the shore, and eventually rising beyond the lake on switchbacks. Lap up the Hell Roaring canyon vistas and engrossing miles ahead on the well-graded trail (rerouted since the 1963 Mount Cramer topo). At Imogene's outlet, 5.9 miles from your start at Hell Roaring upper trailhead, the new trail stays left on the east shore while the old, neglected path shown on the 1963 Snowyside Peak topo goes right. The two meet near the inlet a long mile away. The waters of Imogene are clear and deep, surrounding near-shore islands. The largest "Paradise Lost" has campsites accessible at lower water levels.

From Imogene, use a topo map to find the half-dozen lakes and ponds located off-trail beneath Payette Peak to the southwest, and also to find Profile Lake and a lake nicknamed "Lucille" below Mount Cramer.

Side Trip: Imogene Lake to Imogene Divide
2 miles round trip
Moderate to strenuous
Elevation gain: 800 feet
High point: 9,240 feet

An alternative to cross-country exploring near Imogene is to take the trail from Imogene inlet 1 mile to Imogene Divide (9,240 feet) where you'll overlook the entire Imogene Lake. Southward is emerald Edith Lake and the path leading to Sand Mountain Pass—both key links in longer Sawtooth travels. The north-facing switchbacks through talus to Imogene Divide may have snow until August. The snow means a frisky, rapid descent for competent glissaders.

Hell Roaring Lake and Finger of Fate

Alternative Hike: Hell Roaring Lake to Pettit Lake
15.8 miles one way
Strenuous
Elevation gain: 2,440 feet; loss 2,640 feet

From Imogene Divide, it's 7.9 miles back to upper Hell Roaring trailhead. With advance planning you can go, instead, the same distance, mostly downhill, to Edith Lake, Toxaway canyon, and over the ridge to Pettit Lake (Edith Lake and Toxaway canyon are described in trip 34). You'll need a ride to upper Hell Roaring trailhead and a waiting car at the Tin Cup hiker trailhead at Pettit.

This trek covers over 16 miles of unrepeated wilderness panorama in a day—a well-earned treat for having conditioned your feet and body to withstand the rocky trails. It's a gripping farewell when the point of no return is reached (in this instance, Imogene Divide) and you drop into the unknown lands ahead on the other side. Once committed, there are no short cuts. Since the Toxaway trail is heavily used, you can't get lost. But don't miss the essential turnoff for the ridge trail to Pettit Lake described in trip 34. (Another option that saves 1.2 miles: leave a car at Yellow Belly Lake. But allow extra time to shuttle a vehicle there over the rough Yellow Belly Road.)

Pettit Lake

SAWTOOTH NATIONAL FOREST
Sawtooth National Recreation Area

31 PETTIT LAKE HIKES

Best for: hiking
1.6 miles to 5 miles round trip
Easy to moderate
Elevation gain: negligible except hikes 4 and 5
High point: 7,520 feet
Hikable: late May through October
Maps: USGS Alturas Lake, Snowyside Peak

Volunteers at work on the Pettit Lake inlet path

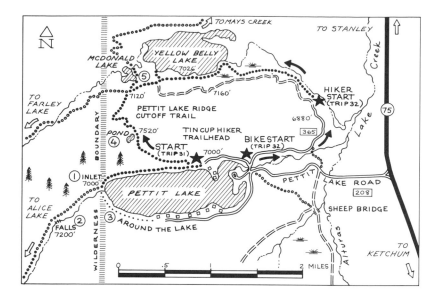

Reach Pettit Lake access road 43.7 miles north from Ketchum via Highway 75, or 18.2 miles south from Stanley. At the signed turnoff, scan the Pleistocene geology: the sage and tree-dotted ridges ahead are glacial moraines made of rock and dirt scraped from the mountains by ice. Pettit Lake lies beyond the terminal moraine at the foot of glacier-carved, U-shaped Pettit Lake canyon. Just to the north is Toxaway canyon, similarly formed and with a similar lake (Yellow Belly, trip 32) at its mouth.

From Highway 75, drive two infamous washboard miles to Pettit Lake and go right at the first junction. Cross the outlet bridge, and stay left to Tin Cup hiker trailhead where there are restrooms and a much-appreciated water pump.

Hike 1: Tin Cup to Pettit Lake Inlet
2.4 miles round trip
Easy

Start at Tin Cup trailhead, sign in at the trail registry (important even for a short hike because hiker counts influence trail budgets), and strike out on an easy stroll along Pettit Lake's timbered north shore. Shortly after leaving Tin Cup, a path from a horse transfer camp joins the main trail. At 0.2 mile, pass a fork going right, uphill, to McDonald Lake and Toxaway canyon. Keep meandering through Douglas fir and lodgepole pine until lake's end near the wilderness boundary sign. Then go left on a faint path toward the driftwood beach. The main trail continues toward Alice Lake. From water's edge, look back the length of Pettit to the yonder White Cloud Mountains, a scene enriched by sunset hues.

Hike 2: Tin Cup to Pettit Lake Creek Falls
4 miles round trip
Easy

Follow hike 1 to the wilderness boundary sign at 1.2 miles, and proceed on the Alice Lake trail. Walk through a lush forest, cool and fragrant on the hottest of days, and go by a granite rockslide on the side of Parks Peak. You're away from the creek until approaching the cascading falls at 2 miles.

Hike 3: Around-the-Lake Loop
4.3 miles
Easy, except for inlet section

Circling Pettit Lake involves two parts road, one part trail, and one part bushwhack at the inlet. Use directions in hike 1 to reach the lake's far end. Leave the main trail by the wilderness boundary, bear left, and take a primitive path disappearing into the green tangle ahead. In 1988, Pettit Lake homeowners pruned and hand-sawed a route through the 0.3 mile of inlet jungle. But you may still have to duck limbs, skirt bogs, and balance across conveniently toppled trees to bridge the two inlet streams. Once out of the thickest growth, a well-defined path goes 0.6 mile to the summer cabins on the south shore and joins the lake road to go 2.1 miles back to Tin Cup. (Note: Please, no summer campfires at the densely wooded inlet, where a spark could set the forest ablaze.)

Hike 4: Tin Cup Trailhead to Pettit Lake Ridge
1.6 miles round trip
Easy
Elevation gain: 520 feet

An upward hike leads to loftier views of Pettit Lake, Alice Lake canyon, McDonald Peak, and Parks Peak, and ends at a hidden pond at Pettit Lake ridge. From Tin Cup, walk 0.2 mile to the signed trail going right, toward McDonald and Yellow Belly lakes. Climb steadily on dusty, rocky trail through open timber, taking long looks southward toward the lakes and peaks as clearings permit. When the path levels at 0.8 mile, look for the grass-enshrouded pond off the trail to the left.

Hike 5: Tin Cup over Pettit Lake Ridge to McDonald Lake and Yellow Belly Lake
5 miles round trip
Easy
Elevation gain: 520 feet; loss 400 feet

Take hike 4 up to Pettit Lake ridge and then descend to Toxaway canyon trail at 1.8 miles—stepping over 59 log waterbars on the way. Turn right and go 30 yards to a signed path leading 250 yards to the burned eastern shoreline of McDonald Lake. Look south across the shallow, marshy lake for views up Toxaway canyon. From McDonald Lake it's just a level 0.5 mile to larger

A yearling cub at Tin Cup trailhead

Yellow Belly Lake. To see it, rejoin the Toxaway trail, turn left, and descend to Yellow Belly; a path leads along the lake's eastern shoreline. Return to Pettit Lake by retracing your route to Tin Cup over Pettit Lake Ridge. (Or take a longer trip back to Pettit Lake and Tin Cup trailhead via Yellow Belly trail and road, about 3.8 miles (see trip 32, Yellow Belly Lake).

SAWTOOTH NATIONAL FOREST
Sawtooth National Recreation Area

32 YELLOW BELLY LAKE

Best for: hiking
Opportunities for: mountain biking, scenic drive
2.6 miles round trip
Easy
Elevation gain: 280 feet
High point: 7,160 feet
Hikable: June through October
Maps: USGS Alturas Lake, Snowyside Peak, Obsidian,
    Mount Cramer

Yellow Belly Lake is a sizeable 188 acres and lies at the mouth of Toxaway canyon. Yellow Belly, along with its neighbor, McDonald Lake, is close to Pettit Lake via a rough 3.4-mile road. A foothill setting allows early-season hiking or sheltered walks on rainy days. Both are gateways to the alpine treasureland in Toxaway canyon (trip 34). And Yellow Belly Lake has fish (it is closed to motorboats; a canoe is helpful).

The Forest Service has laid out a new future of improved road and trails for the Yellow Belly area, planned to unfold in the early 1990s. At present the final 2 miles of road is over morainal rocks hidden by powdery dust. Check with SNRA Ranger Stations for an update.

Follow directions to Pettit Lake, trip 31, to the outlet bridge where a bike ride could start. Go right (northeast) on Yellow Belly Road 365, up a small hill, and at 0.5 mile, climb another hill. At 0.6 mile, a knoll provides far-reaching views of the Sawtooth Valley and White Cloud foothills—ride this far just for sunset-watching. Drop down a twisting corner (a hard pedal on the return) and reach a sagebrush clearing at 0.8 mile; the road borders the clearing. Near 1.4 miles, as the route begins to climb, look for faint wheel tracks going toward Yellow Belly Creek (which is hidden by trees).

Begin a hike where the trail starts along the stream—there is currently no sign. Whether you're hiking, biking, or driving, walk over to Yellow Belly Creek and go up the path 0.1 mile. Through a primeval forest, Yellow Belly Creek rushes in hell-roaring fashion, especially in May and June, over a wide swath of bleached granite boulders.

Hikers can continue up the path 1.3 miles to Yellow Belly outlet. Drivers with low-clearance cars should park here and also take the trail. Experienced mountain bikers may ride the path, which starts out rough before improving. On the road it's another 2 miles to the lake.

At Yellow Belly a trail goes along the south shore between the outlet and trailhead. The lake has a north woods ambience, although when you look from the outlet southwest across the water to crags up Toxaway canyon you'll be reminded—this *is* Idaho, not Minnesota. From the opposite shoreline, the view is northeast toward the White Cloud Mountain foothills.

Side Trip: Yellow Belly to McDonald Lake

> 1.0 mile round trip
> Easy
> Elevation gain: 40 feet
> High point: 7,120 feet
> Map: USGS Snowyside Peak

Serene little McDonald Lake is just 0.5 mile away by nearly level trail. The route is closed to motorcycles, but not to bicycles until the wilderness boundary 0.2 mile beyond McDonald Lake. As you approach marshy McDonald Lake a path goes right, 0.1 mile through a charred forest to the shoreline. The dead trees are a reminder to be careful with campfires and cigarettes. Campsites are scarce due to swamp and deadfall.

Taking a wet shortcut through Pettit Lake Creek to Yellow Belly Road

From McDonald Lake, hikers can make a loop by going 1.8 miles back to Pettit Lake. When you leave McDonald Lake go right for 30 yards on the Toxaway canyon trail, then go left on the Pettit Lake ridge cutoff trail (see trip 31, hike 5). This route's not recommended for bicyclists, as the section from Toxaway canyon trail to the ridgetop has a 420-foot elevation gain and 59 log waterbars that were not designed for wheels.

33 ALICE LAKE, SNOWYSIDE PASS

Best for: hiking
11 miles round trip
Strenuous
Elevation gain: 1,600 feet
High point: 8,600 feet
Hikable: July through October
Map: USGS Snowyside Peak

Turnaround at "Halfway Pond"

6 miles round trip
Moderate
Elevation gain: 520 feet
High point: 7,520 feet

Alice Lake has won the lug-soled vote as the Sawtooth's leading lady. Like most superstars she is extolled, photographed, and seldom left alone.

Alice Lake trail

Alice Lake is not an easy hike; it's 5.5 miles one way, gaining 1,600 feet in elevation. For many hikers it's a first wilderness trek—a foot-battering initiation to a wild land of snowy peaks, silvery pools, granite islands, and alpine flowers.

The hike begins at Pettit Lake's Tin Cup hiker trailhead. See trip 31, walk 2, for access and trail description as far as the waterfall at 2 miles. The trail continues through forest and crosses the creek on logs twice in the next mile. Some wading may be necessary, and early in the season the high water may be impassable.

At 3 miles, halfway to Alice, there's a shallow pond below the trail, just before the path starts up a series of boulder-field switchbacks beneath Parks Peak. The loggy pond and surrounding high country views can be a short hike's destination—most longer-distance trekkers don't have time to stop to explore this locale. At this halfway point you've gained 500 feet since Pettit Lake and have another 1,100 feet to go. Alice Lake lies in the canyon above to the right (southwest); an unnamed, trailless drainage is due south.

The trail to Alice continues upward through an increasingly untamed land. El Capitan towers in the south. Alice Lake Creek is crossed three more times on log jams or by bridge. At 5.5 miles, pass two mirror-like ponds, reflecting alpine firs and alpine peaks, and walk on to Alice a few yards away. There are plentiful campsites.

Side Trip: Alice Lake to Twin Lakes and Snowyside Pass

> 4 miles round trip
> Strenuous
> Elevation gain: 760 feet
> High point: 9,400 feet
> Hikable: mid-July through September

At 6 miles, the trail to Twin Lakes and Snowyside Pass leaves Alice and climbs west a mile, gaining 260 feet to the matched pair of lakes beneath Snowyside Peak. Most day hikers stop here unless planning a loop using Toxaway canyon (see below).

Past Twin Lakes, a long mile of trail climbs over 500 feet to Snowyside Pass (9,400 feet) at 8 miles. This is a gain of 2,360 feet from Pettit Lake Tin Cup trailhead. The final spine-tingling section to the pass has been carved from rock (new trail not shown on the 1964 Snowyside topo). From Snowyside Pass, look upon a wild masterwork—Twin Lakes and Snowyside Peak. In the other direction, to the northwest, lie more lakes, more mountains, and the route to Toxaway Lake.

Alternative Hike: Alice–Toxaway Loop

> 17 miles
> Strenuous
> Elevation gain: 2,800 feet, loss 2,900 feet
> High point: 9,400 feet
> Hikable: mid-July through September

Trail near Snowyside Pass above Twin Lakes

The Sawtooth's number-one weekend backpacking loop is also a long day hike. After reaching Snowyside Pass at 8 miles, the trail drops 2 miles to Toxaway Lake, passes around the lake's shoreline for a mile, and goes 7 miles back to Pettit Lake via Toxaway canyon and Pettit Lake ridge cutoff trail (described in trip 31, hike 5). Snow that may block the trail until August stays longer on the north (Toxaway) side of Snowyside Pass.

There are pros and cons on which direction to do in the loop. Elevation gain and loss is the same in either direction. However, going up Toxaway drainage is a more gradual climb and saves the views of Twin Lakes and Snowyside Peak for the trip's last half. By going out Alice Lake canyon to Pettit Lake, the last portion of the trip is all downhill. A Toxaway canyon exit requires a 400-foot climb back over the cutoff trail to Pettit at day's end—when you reach this point you'll wish you had done the loop counterclockwise instead.

SAWTOOTH NATIONAL FOREST
Sawtooth Wilderness

34 TOXAWAY CANYON HIKES

Best for: hiking
6 miles to 12 miles round trip; 15.3-mile loop
Moderate to strenuous
Elevation gain: 720 feet to 2,320 feet
Hikable: July through October
Map: USGS Snowyside Peak

The easiest acquaintance with Toxaway canyon is a 6-mile round trip from Yellow Belly Lake to Farley Lake. Go about twice that distance and the reward is either Edith Lake or Toxaway Lake. An ambitious 15-mile loop takes you by Toxaway to Sand Mountain Pass to Edith Lake and back home. Wherever you go in July and August you'll be sharing the trail with others, especially horsemen and packstock headed for Toxaway Lake.

Toxaway canyon is reached either from Pettit Lake Tin Cup hiker trailhead (see trip 31, hike 5) or Yellow Belly Lake trailhead (trip 32). The distances and elevation gains described here are from Yellow Belly, reachable by high-clearance vehicle. A word about these two trailheads' logistics when planning Toxaway canyon hikes. The essence: beginning at Yellow Belly rather than Tin Cup lessens the hiking distance to Farley, Edith, or Toxaway lakes by 2.4 miles round trip and saves 930 feet in elevation change. Despite this, many hikers prefer starting at Tin Cup and walking over Pettit Lake ridge cutoff to Toxaway canyon trail in order to avoid driving the rough Yellow Belly Lake Road. This may change if scheduled road improvements take place.

If you begin at Tin Cup, add 1.2 miles each way to the Toxaway canyon trips described here and watch closely for the Pettit Lake ridge cutoff trail on your return at day's end. (If you pass by burned forest near McDonald Lake, you missed the turnoff.)

Farley Lake

> 6 miles round trip
> Moderate
> Elevation gain: 720 feet
> High point: 7,800 feet

Follow description in trip 32 to drive from Pettit Lake to Yellow Belly Lake trailhead. Take the signed Toxaway canyon trail toward Farley Lake. At 0.5 mile, a path leads right 200 yards through burned trees to McDonald Lake. In just 30 yards the Toxaway canyon trail is joined by the Pettit Lake ridge cutoff trail. At 0.7 mile, enter the wilderness boundary and at 1.2 miles, reach the hike's most challenging point—a creek crossing on logs (difficult or impassable at high runoff).

Once across, continue walking through forest that gradually gives way to talus slopes, meadows, and cascading streams. Parks Peak is to the south, Imogene Peak to the north. As you climb higher, look back at Yellow Belly Lake. Castle Peak rises over the distant White Clouds to the east.

Underfoot the excellent canyon trail is the result of reconstruction in 1988. At 3 miles, side paths go to overlooks of Farley Lake and a few limited campsites. Families with children should be cautious around Farley Lake's steep shoreline.

Edith Lake

> 11.2 miles round trip
> Moderate
> Elevation gain: 1,600 feet
> High point: 8,680 feet

From Yellow Belly trailhead it's 4.6 miles to Edith Lake junction. Look closely for the weathered sign and easy-to-miss path going right. The scenic 1-mile trail gains 480 feet, traversing stream-washed granite slabs to reach windswept Edith Lake and a handful of campsites. From the lake it's a rocky 0.5 mile to the signed junction with the Imogene Divide–Sand Mountain Pass trail and two mouth-watering choices (with an early start, both can be done in the same day). Go right (north) to climb the 0.5-mile-long switchbacks to Imogene Divide (9,240 feet), and view of Imogene Lake (see trip 30).

A left (south) turn at the junction leads up the Sand Mountain Pass trail. Go a mile until views of the South Fork Payette drainage appear to the west. Below is "Rendezvous Lake" (an unofficial name); in the distance is Virginia Lake. A short scramble to the east ridgetop brings a superb overlook of Toxaway Lake to the south. Below to the northeast is Edith, Farley, and Yellow Belly lakes. Such sights make it hard to go home.

Note: For strong hikers headed to the backpacking destinations of Edna, Virginia, Vernon, or Ardeth lakes (which are often accessed via Sand Mountain Pass), Edith Lake cutoff is the shortest route. This route is 7 miles to Sand Mountain Pass from Yellow Belly Lake. This shortcut traverses a precipitous, sloughing section on Sand Mountain's west side that can be avoided, however, by using the wider, more gradual switchback trail from Toxaway Lake to Sand Mountain Pass (see below).

Toxaway Lake

> 12 miles round trip
> Strenuous
> Elevation gain: 1,320 feet
> High point: 8,400 feet

Toxaway Lake is 6 miles from Yellow Belly trailhead and a modest elevation gain of 1,200 feet. End to end, Toxaway Lake is over a mile long with nooks and crannies galore. The path stays well above the lake, but wander from it for closer looks at the granite "wizard" island and at Snowyside Peak to the southwest. There are numerous campsites.

At Toxaway's southern end, the canyon beneath Snowyside Peak provides a 2-mile-long, 1,000-foot ascent to Snowyside Pass, where you're never quite ready for the startling, bewitching sight of Twin Lakes below, nor for the initial cliffhanging descent to reach them. The trail from Toxaway to the pass has been rerouted since the 1964 Snowyside topo. For a description of the Alice–Toxaway Loop hike see trip 33.

Toxaway–Edith Lake Loop

> 15.3 miles
> Strenuous
> Elevation gain: 2,320 feet
> High point: 9,400 feet
> Hikable: late July through September

An all-day trek for experienced hikers goes from Toxaway Lake up 2 miles on gradual switchbacks to Sand Mountain Pass, 8.3 miles from Yellow Belly Lake. As you climb to the pass you'll have a superb view of Toxaway Lake and Snowyside Peak plus, from the pass, a look west to the South Fork Payette River country.

From the pass, take the signed trail to Edith Lake. Before the path starts to descend into the lake basin, leave it and scramble upward to the ridgetop for views of Toxaway Lake to the south and Edith, Farley, and Yellow Belly lakes to the northeast. Picture-taking completed, reach Edith Lake at 9.8 miles and continue downward to the Toxaway canyon trail at 10. 8 miles. Return the final 4.6 miles to Yellow Belly trailhead.

Toxaway Lake from Sand Mountain Pass trail

Alturas Lake

35 ALTURAS LAKE CREEK

Best for: mountain biking
5.8-mile loop
Easy
Elevation gain: negligible
High point: 7,040 feet
Riding surface: dirt, gravel, pavement
Ridable: mid-May through October
Maps: USGS Alturas Lake, Snowyside Peak

An easy-wheeling loop begins at Alturas Lake and follows back roads through dandelion-filled meadows and deer- and elk-laden forest. Take this trip early in the season (May into June) and you'll splash for nearly 0.5 mile through a

Alturas Lake Creek near Perkins Lake

wayward stream spilling down the firm gravel roadbed. Wear your "splattering" clothes (kids love this ride).

This loop and the next five bikes and hikes to follow (trips 36–40) are reason for car campers to use Alturas Lake as a base. At 838 acres, Alturas Lake is the Sawtooth's second largest. A paved road leads halfway around Alturas to campgrounds and beach areas. Alturas Lake Road 205 is 40.7 miles north of Ketchum on Highway 75; 21.1 miles south of Stanley. To begin the ride, drive 2.5 miles to the first Alturas Lake Picnic Area, just past the bridge over the lake's outlet stream. The Alturas Lake Lodge shown on the 1963 USGS map is gone.

You're embarking on a route easy to find once ridden, but unmarked roads may be confusing the first time so read directions closely. From the picnic area continue on Alturas Road 0.4 mile and turn right on graveled Cabin Creek Road 207. If recently graded, Cabin Creek Road may temporarily lack its notorious washboards. Otherwise, hang on, and near 0.7 mile, cross a small stream. An old cabin is visible to the right (east). At 0.8 mile, just past a powerline, look for an unsigned, faint track going through the grass. The track almost immediately becomes a distinct road and leads to several buildings at an old homestead at 1 mile. This road is shown on the 1963 Alturas Lake topo. If, on Cabin Creek Road, you reach a sign for Cabin Creek Organization Camp or Cabin Creek trailhead, you missed the turn.

Among the pioneer ruins are tin-roofed, chinked log cabins that were rescued when Alturas Lake Lodge and outbuildings were removed. Past the cabins find the 0.5 mile of "splash alley." In late spring the water runs several inches deep down both tire tracks of the road. Splash on! Or ride on the edge of the road and stay dry.

At 1.5 miles, stay left (the other two choices are dead ends) and go 200 yards (possibly through large, deep mud puddles) until you're almost back to Cabin Creek Road, which you'll see 50 yards away. Instead of rejoining Cabin Creek Road turn right on a well-used dirt road (not shown on forest or USGS maps) that leads to shallow Alturas Lake Creek and a pole footbridge at 2.5 miles.

Cross the bridge and follow a well-traveled, hummocky road as it climbs a knoll and intersects a road going left at 2.7 miles. Stay right, dropping off the knoll, heading back toward the creek and then bending left and heading out through lodgepole pines to join the paved Alturas Lake Road at 3.6 miles. Go right. In 0.5 mile you'll pass a lovely meadow. Look for deer and sandhill cranes. Pass by public access roads to Perkins Lake at 4.9 and 5.3 miles, and reach Alturas Lake at 5.8 miles.

SAWTOOTH NATIONAL FOREST
Sawtooth National Recreation Area

36 ALTURAS LAKE TO PETTIT LAKE

Best for: mountain biking
12.2 miles round trip
Easy to moderate
Elevation gain: 120 feet
High point: 7,000 feet
Riding surface: dirt, gravel, cobble roads
Ridable: May through October
Maps: USGS Alturas Lake, Snowyside Peak

With some zigzagging and backtracking, a backroads route, all on public land, can be ridden from Alturas Lake to Pettit Lake (or vice-versa; the directions here start at Alturas Lake). The wide Sawtooth Valley floor is a friendly conditioner for early-season muscles or for visitors unused to high altitudes. If possible, ride lake-to-lake in technicolor June, when the 'tooths are still winter white, when wheels spray through snowmelt puddles, and penstemon, geraniums, and bluebells still blanket the sheep meadows. There's only one notable hill, but the ride's distance is a bit long for youngsters.

See trip 35 (Alturas Lake Creek) for access to the Alturas Lake Picnic area closest to the outlet stream where this ride begins. Follow trip 35 for the first 1.5 miles as it takes the scenic detour by the homestead site, but rejoin Cabin Creek Road 207 instead of heading right to the pole bridge. Once back on Cabin Creek Road at 1.6 miles, pedal north (right), up a small hill, and at 2.3 miles, turn right (east) on a powerline road (not shown on 1963 topo). Like

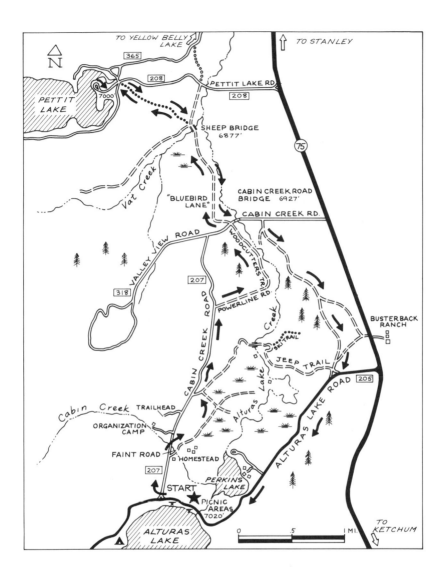

the homestead detour earlier, this side road is taken to escape Cabin Creek Road's dust and corrugated surface (though it has some cobbles of its own). At 3.0 miles, reach the shore of Alturas Lake Creek and join a woodcutter's primitive road going left.

The next 0.8 mile is mostly dirt, though stumps and river rock provide slalom practice. At 3.8 miles, leave the road and meet up with Cabin Creek Road near where it bridges Alturas Lake Creek.

To continue biking toward Pettit Lake, don't cross the bridge. Look for a

The Vat Creek sheep bridge on the lake-to-lake route

dirt road just ahead of where you exited the woods and met Cabin Creek Road. Go left (west) on the dirt road, through a 100-yard-long lodgepole pine archway, and then angle around a wire fence and head due north on "Bluebird Lane." This lane goes 1.1 miles to a photogenic, rustic sheep bridge over Vat Creek at 5 miles.

Immediately after the bridge is a three-way intersection. Your route to Pettit Lake is the center choice. A trail goes 0.8 mile up a swale and over the ridge to Pettit Lake at 5.8 miles. This trail is also your return route. At Pettit's shore, bask in the sun and cool your feet.

To return to Alturas, take the rollicking descent from the Pettit Lake moraine back to the sheep bridge and go right on "Bluebird Lane" to Cabin Creek Road at 7.8 miles. Go left 20 yards to the Alturas Lake Creek bridge and a different route back to Alturas Lake. Cross the bridge, taking Cabin Creek Road east (toward Highway 75) for 0.4 mile, passing bluebird houses, and turning right on a primitive road, just after crossing a sizeable irrigation stream. Follow the road for 0.2 mile along the left bank of the water and, just past a mudhole, go left at a Y. Ride through sagebrush, skirting the forest. At 9.3 miles, the increasingly cobbly road splits again; veer right (left goes to Highway 75 and Busterback Ranch) and head south for Alturas Lake Road, reaching it at 10 miles. Go right, returning on pavement to Alturas at 12.2 miles.

Side Trip: *Yellow Belly Road*

The road from the sheep bridge going right (north) leads a level 0.5 mile to Pettit Lake Road 208. Connect to Yellow Belly Lake Road 365 by crossing road 208 and following a faint jeep trail (veer left when it splits into a Y) to rushing Pettit Lake Creek in 0.2 mile. Ford the bouldery stream (wadable by mid-July) and go 0.2 mile to meet Yellow Belly Road at 0.9 mile from Pettit Lake. Continue right to Yellow Belly Lake (see trip 32) or left back to Pettit.

SAWTOOTH NATIONAL FOREST
Sawtooth National Recreation Area

37 ALTURAS LAKE SOUTH SHORE

Best for: hiking
Easy
4.4 miles round trip
Elevation gain: negligible
High point: 7,040 feet
Hikable: late May through October
Map: USGS Alturas Lake

A primitive woodland path along Alturas Lake's south shore is a 10-plus nature trail for hikers. Begin at Alturas Lake Picnic Area, closest to the outlet

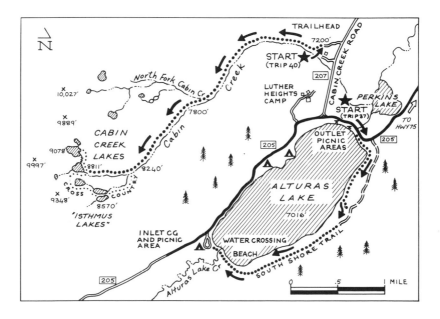

bridge (see trip 35 for directions). Use the nearby bridge to cross Alturas Lake Creek outlet and turn right toward the lake. There's also a small parking area for a few cars on the east side of the bridge. Look for a trail going toward the sandy shore.

Walk east on the beach and enjoy views the length of Alturas. At 0.2 mile, the path enters trees along the lake's south shore. At 0.4 mile, it temporarily leaves the lake and joins a primitive road (closed to motorized use) at 0.5 mile. Note this log-lined intersection at the bottom of a hill on the old road. You'll want to use the lakeside trail on the return. The road becomes a trail at 0.7 mile and the forest closes in.

For the next 1.5 miles to lake's end, the soft, spongy path goes through a pleasant lakeside jungle of alders and willows, grandfather Douglas firs, and younger lodgepole pines. The rich, damp understory is a profusion of blossoms. For the most solitude and quiet lakeside picnics, come midweek or during inclement weather that discourages power boaters or jet skiers on the water. Before mid-June and after Labor Day are usually other peaceful times.

At the upper end of the lake at 2.2 miles, the path goes down to the beach; this is the turnaround point if you're hiking back to the outlet picnic area.

Alternative Hike: South Shore Trail
        2.4 miles one way
        Moderate (stream crossing)

Canada goose at Alturas Lake

By mid- to late June a one-way hike with a refreshing stream crossing can be done on the South Shore trail from Outlet Picnic Area to Inlet Picnic Area (or vice-versa). Until then, the water of Alturas Lake Creek inlet may be too deep for the required ford.

Use directions above to lake's end at 2.2 miles. Walk the shore another 0.2 mile and maneuver through willows to reach the placid inlet stream. A sandbar extends into the lake, but the water near the south bank is thigh deep. Wade across—the footing is solid on the sandy bottom. Once on the other bank, a soggy path goes 100 yards to the popular Inlet Picnic Area, where you can meet a shuttled car or bicycle.

If you're unsure of the cold, deep wade and prefer a one-way hike, begin at the inlet and face the water crossing first. When hiking from inlet to outlet, watch closely on the old road section at 1.9 miles for the trail turnoff which takes you back to the lakeshore. If you start going up a sharp hill, you've missed the turn. The old road eventually joins Alturas Lake Road 0.3 mile from Outlet Picnic Area.

SAWTOOTH NATIONAL FOREST
Sawtooth Wilderness

38 ALPINE CREEK KNOLL

Best for: hiking
Easy to moderate
2 miles round trip
Elevation gain: 406 feet
High point: 7,486 feet
Hikable: June through October
Map: USGS Snowyside Peak

A short walk leads to a granite knoll amid rugged surroundings in Alpine Creek canyon in the Sawtooth Wilderness near Alturas Lake. The high country above Alturas is less known than other Sawtooth destinations, a fact cherished by the region's admirers who say little about their secret haunts here. Rugged, upper Alpine Creek with north and south drainages is managed as trailless (primitive paths that do exist are not maintained).

From Alturas Lake Outlet Picnic Area, drive or bicycle the paved 2.4-mile length of the lake and go another 1.7 miles on dirt and rock road to the unmarked Alpine Creek trailhead located in forest by a ford of Alpine Creek (a winsome trailhead—small, shady, unimproved). Look for a sign pointing west to Alpine Creek trail (don't cross the nearby footbridge for this outing, a common mistake of hikers new to this area). After a few hundred yards arrive at a trail register by the wilderness boundary.

For the next mile, walk upward in the damp, richly forested canyon. One steep, eroded section requires effort, otherwise the walking is mild. Leave the timber, and the imposing, bare northern ridge of Alpine Creek begins to appear. As the canyon widens watch left for a pink granite knoll prominent enough to

View from Alpine Creek Knoll

rank an elevation notation (7,486 feet) on the Snowyside topo map. Climb aboard for a loftier perch to mountain watch.

Below the outcropping's precipitous backside (watch youngsters closely) Alpine Creek winds through emerald grass. A cascade is heard but unseen. Far to the east, Eureka Gulch and Jake's Gulch rise out of Alturas Lake Creek canyon. Over the inviting, gnarly north ridge lie Cabin Creek Lakes (trip 40).

Beyond the knoll the remaining 1.7 miles of Alpine Creek trail are infrequently maintained.

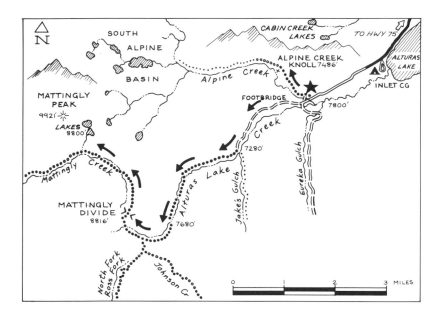

SAWTOOTH NATIONAL FOREST
Sawtooth Wilderness

39 MATTINGLY CREEK

Best for: hiking
Strenuous
15 miles round trip
Elevation gain: 1,736 feet
High point: 8,816 feet
Hikable: July through October
Maps: USGS Snowyside Peak, Marshall Peak

A dedicated 6-mile hike is necessary just to reach Mattingly Divide, the canyon's headgate. Then more walking, more work is necessary to unravel Mattingly's secrets. A day hike to Mattingly is most appreciated by hikers willing to cover

Mapping out the next adventure in Mattingly Creek

14 to 16 miles from sunup to sundown and take off cross-country for more adventures.

The trip begins at the Alpine Creek trailhead above Alturas Lake. See directions in trip 35 to reach Alturas Lake, and in trip 38 for Alpine Creek trailhead. Cross the footbridge near the trailhead and continue straight on the dirt road (bypassing at 0.2 mile the left turn to Eureka Gulch) and reach a registration box at 2.2 miles.

Past the sign-in box, the road becomes a trail and climbs mildly 400 feet in 2.2 miles, through an avalanche-swept open canyon, to a ford of Alturas Lake Creek. This first 4.4 miles is an easy hike. Presently motorbikes are allowed. Beyond the stream the steep, wet mountainside trail climbs a grueling 1,000 feet in 1.5 miles to reach Mattingly Divide (8,816 feet) and the wilderness boundary at 6 miles. The final 0.8 mile is closed to motorbikes.

After the workout to reach Mattingly Divide you expect breathless views, but what you'll see instead are Forest Service signs and a meadow of alpine daisies. A carved wooden survivor of many winters reads: Alturas Lake 10, Middle Fork Boise River Trail 6, and Atlanta 11. From the divide, create your Mattingly adventure. The obvious choice, but not the only one, is continuing on the trail, which plunges into Mattingly Creek canyon, losing nearly 500 feet the first mile, leveling out for 0.3 mile, then losing 700 feet by the end of the second mile. By the time the trail reaches the Middle Fork Boise River 6 miles away the elevation loss is 2,795 feet.

Explore downward, encouraged by pristine parkland and gardens of neon-colored moss. The two lakes are on a shelf 500 feet above the valley floor to the north. Mattingly Peak is the tallest point on the jagged northwest sky-line—far less imposing from this angle than from Spangle Pass deep in the Sawtooths. For scramblers, opportunity is everywhere—ridgetop walks, hidden valleys, new routes home. The lake-rich South Alpine Creek drainage is over the north ridge. Route-finding skills are needed, and energy to match—this wilderness is still wild.

A final note: Mattingly Creek canyon has been treasured by a few and unknown by most. With its out-of-the-way location at the southeastern edge of the Sawtooth Wilderness, it could use more friends to help safeguard its perimeter. Sometimes motorbikes illegally churn to Mattingly Divide and leave tire prints on the meadow. The same friends could come to know and speak for the nearby ecosystem of Johnson Creek, North Fork of Ross Fork, and Vienna Creek in the proposed Smoky Mountain Wilderness.

SAWTOOTH NATIONAL FOREST
Sawtooth Wilderness

40 CABIN CREEK LAKES

Best for: hiking
7.0 miles round trip
Moderate
Elevation gain: 1,731 feet
High point: 8,811 feet
Hikable: late June through October
Maps: USGS Alturas Lake, Snowyside Peak

Reach Cabin Creek trailhead by going to Alturas Lake (see trip 35 for directions) and take Cabin Creek Road 207 for 0.7 mile to the signed road leading left to the trailhead. Park under shade trees and head up a sunny, lupine- and sage-covered hillside to the trail register. The path follows the north side of Cabin Creek canyon, passing at 1.6 miles a side stream from a trailless drainage to the northwest, where shallow lakes and ponds hide beneath a 10,027-foot bare mountain.

Continue on the main Cabin Creek canyon trail, noticing at 2.8 miles where two streams draining from different lakes merge. The path stays right, climbs abruptly, and in 0.5 mile reaches Lake 8811. (If you're using the first edition,

1988, of the 1:48,000 Sawtooth Wilderness colored map, the trail is incorrectly shown leading to the connected "Isthmus Lakes.")

Hikers seeking more isolation can continue to the other four Cabin Creek Lakes. The highest is Lake 9078; its outlet forms a waterfall to Lake 8811 (except in a dry year). Lake 9078 is reached by walking around Lake 8811's east shore and climbing to the right of the falls.

To see the other three lakes, climb from Lake 8811 over the small ridge to the south. You'll first encounter a lake that's more a pool. Further below lie the delightful twin isthmus lakes, separated by a slice of land where an ancient whitebark pine has a tenacious grip. Walk the narrow strip, look out across both lakes at once, and see beyond the western skyline. At one point a tiny channel connects the lakes—cross it on unsteady logs. Below the Siamese lake labeled on the topo as 8570, look for a tiny pond where trees are reflected in silver water and a mud shoreline preserves the comings and goings of night-time visitors. To make a loop and rejoin the main trail, follow the outlet of the northern isthmus lake, staying on the left side of the stream in deep, dark woods to rejoin in 0.3 mile the main path, and descend to the trailhead.

A word to hikers with mountain goat tendencies—there's exploring be-

Lake 8811, Cabin Creek drainage, and the Sawtooth Valley beyond

yond Lake 9078 to a labyrinth of ravines and gnarly granite hummocks. Or scale the western ridge above Lake 8811 and look southwest into spectacular Alpine Creek canyon (you're above the pink granite knoll described in trip 38). Southward from Alpine Creek are views of Alturas Lake Creek canyon, Jake's Gulch, and Eureka Gulch. Northward rise the jutting summits of El Capitan and the lost valley at its eastern flank.

Upper Sawtooth Valley

SAWTOOTH NATIONAL FOREST
Sawtooth National Recreation Area

41 SAWTOOTH CITY

Best for: mountain biking
Opportunities for: scenic drive, hiking
6-mile loop
Easy
Elevation gain: 191 feet
High point: 7,357 feet
Riding surface: gravel and dirt roads
Ridable: June through October
Map: USGS Alturas Lake

To reach historical Sawtooth City—a boom town in the early 1880s—take Highway 75 north of Ketchum to Beaver Creek Road 204 at 37.8 miles and a sign for Sawtooth City ghost town. (From Stanley, go south 24 miles on Highway 75 to Beaver Creek Road.) Parking for bicyclists is near the turnoff.

Sawtooth City is just 2.3 miles away by a bumpy road that climbs slightly to the old townsite. There by the old blacksmith shop a sign simply states the town's years of existence, 1879–1884. Bicycle the few dirt streets searching for remnants (old timers recall when curtains still hung in the cabin windows). The millsite, with a section of hand-laid rock wall, is 0.8 mile up the main road beyond the sign. From the mill ruins is a view of green meadows and upper Beaver Creek canyon where the road continues to the Silver King and Pilgrim mines (see below).

The Sawtooth City cemetery is on a hilltop reached by a short, steep dirt road 0.3 mile east of the historical sign.

From Sawtooth City complete a biking loop using the old wagon way toward Smiley Creek. By the cemetery turnoff, another road leads south, down to a crossing of rocks or logs on Beaver Creek (steep banks prevent vehicle use). High water in May or early June may thwart your loop plans. The old road continues, climbing uphill to a fork. Go straight (east). (The right fork goes to a duck pond; see below.)

The woods give way to sagebrush and the throne-shaped mountain called Abe's Chair looms south. At 0.7 and 0.9 mile past the Beaver Creek crossing,

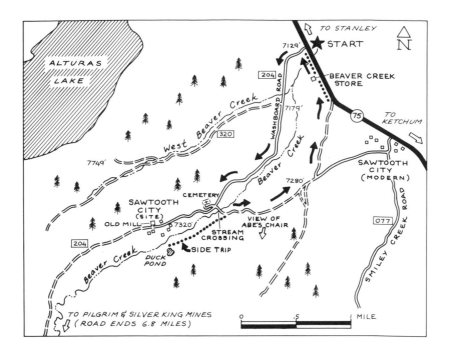

roads go south toward Abe's Chair and Little Beaver Creek. At 1 mile, take a well-defined road going left (north) which leads 0.7 mile to Highway 75 near Beaver Creek Store. From the store, go 0.4 mile on a trail along Highway 75 back to the start at Beaver Creek Road. Next time, ride the loop in reverse. The wagon road is a more scenic entrance to the old ghost town, and Beaver Creek Road is an easier ride going downhill back to Highway 75.

Side Trip to Duck Pond
> 1.6 miles round trip
> Easy

After you cross Beaver Creek and climb the short hill, take the logging trail going right. Follow it 0.3 mile past a recent pole-sale cutting to a clearing. Go right, across the grass, on a faint track which again becomes a distinct road. In another 0.5 mile look for a woodland pond to the left (south). In the drought year of 1988 the pond was mud from shore to shore, but a year later, after a more normal winter snowfall, the pond was nearly full of water and enlivened with ducks.

Alternate Ride: Sawtooth City to Beaver Creek Road's End
> 13.6 miles round trip
> Moderate
> Elevation gain: 680 feet

138

Bicyclists and high-clearance vehicles can continue from Sawtooth City on Beaver Creek Road, passing beaver ponds, avalanche paths, and the old Silver King and Pilgrim mines to road's end at 6.8 miles. If mine work is occurring, the scenic, primitive road may be rockier and dustier than usual. For hikers, game trails lead to ridges nearing 10,000 feet in the upper canyon.

Unmarked grave at Sawtooth City cemetery

42 SMILEY CREEK CANYON, VIENNA

Best for: mountain biking
Opportunities for: scenic drive, hiking
14 miles round trip
Moderate
Elevation gain: 420 feet
High point: 7,600 feet
Riding surface: gravel, dirt, rock
Ridable: June through October
Map: USGS Frenchman Creek

Century-old handhewn timbers left in the woods when the Vienna mines closed

Bike or drive to Vienna City vicinity and explore onward by foot. Little remains of the 200 buildings that once stood here. The 7-mile one-way distance is a moderate cycling workout for adults, but too long for youngsters (they would enjoy coasting back down Smiley Creek canyon from Vienna). The road has rocky and washboard stretches.

The trip begins at Smiley Creek Lodge 37.6 miles from Ketchum via Highway 75. From Stanley, drive south on Highway 75 for 24.2 miles. Near the store are two weathered, inanimate mascots: a mother grizzly and her cub. The big bear has grasp of a salmon, a reminder of the days when the bears fed well on opulent runs of salmon in the nearby streams.

Leave the bears and pedal (or drive) 0.1 mile north on Highway 75, crossing Smiley Creek by bridge, and turn left at the sign for Smiley Creek Road 077. At 2.1 miles the Smiley Creek truck route from Highway 75 joins your route up the canyon.

In another 0.5 mile, see green meadows stretching up the valley for the next 2 miles. Kids of all ages will enjoy the meandering creek and views south of a craggy mountain—locally called Goat Rocks for the beasts that sometimes winter there.

At 5.8 miles the road bridges Smiley Creek. At 7 miles arrive at the site of Vienna City. One log cabin and parts of others remain. A rough mining road continues up the canyon's right fork, passing in 0.25 mile millsite ruins and a giant iron boiler, and reaching a locked gate in 0.5 mile (beyond the gate is patented, or private, land).

To observe the aging stacks of handhewn posts left behind when Vienna City died, take the signed trail to West Fork Big Smoky Creek and Emma Creek, 0.1 mile up the road from the historical sign. Walk a log or wade boot-high Smiley Creek and start uphill. Within 0.25 mile you'll notice the century-old cut wood. Incredible muscle and sweat forged one pile of five rows stretching 100 feet. Ax marks are still vivid. Atop the stacks, tiny firs have taken root on their ancestor's dust.

SAWTOOTH NATIONAL FOREST
Sawtooth National Recreation Area

43 GALENA WAGON ROAD

Best for: mountain biking
Opportunity for: scenic drive, hiking
3.7 miles one way
Easy
Elevation loss: 1,160 feet
High point: 8,640 feet
Riding surface: dirt road
Ridable: June through October
Maps: USGS Galena, Frenchman Creek

For a mountain biking entrance to the Sawtooth Valley, leave from near the Galena Summit area (8,701 feet) and use the 3.7-mile old wagon road to the valley floor. Biking the toll road is an easy prologue to other nearby bike trips, including Headwaters canyon (below) and trips 41 through 46.

From Ketchum, take Highway 75 north over Galena Summit, start to descend, and at 30.2 miles, look right (north) for a wide pullout. The wagon way (road 220) begins across the pavement to the south. Watch for traffic. From Stanley, it's 31.6 miles south via Highway 75 to this point. Unless you've

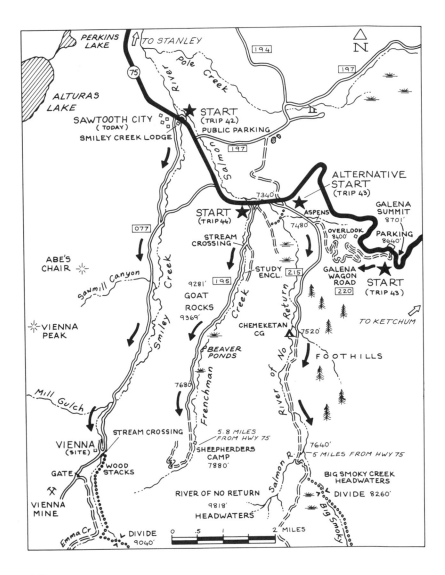

Chamber music in Headwaters canyon

commandeered a driver, draw straws to see which unlucky person has to shuttle the car to the base of the hill.

The old switchback road loses 960 feet as it weaves back and forth through lupine, sunflowers, sagebrush, and forest. Upper Sawtooth Valley views steadily evolve, the Sawtooth peaks tower to the west. At present the old road can be driven by a high-clearance vehicle. Be certain snowbanks are long gone and the roadbed is dry. Hikers can enjoy this trip, too, and a walk (shorter by a mile) could begin at Galena Overlook, since the old road traverses the hillside just below.

At 3.7 miles, reach Camp Creek on Salmon River Road 215 in Headwaters canyon, 1 mile south of Highway 75. Decide the next move, either left, up Headwaters canyon, or turn right, to the highway. Meet your shuttle car there or venture on to other nearby rides.

Side Trip: Headwaters Canyon

> 10 miles round trip (from Highway 75)
> Easy to moderate (stream crossings)
> Elevation gain: 300 feet
> High point: 7,640 feet
> Riding surface: gravel and dirt road

Begin this ride either from Highway 75 at the base of Galena Summit on Salmon River Road 215, or continue from the Galena Wagon Road and Camp Creek described above. (The distance will be 8 miles round trip from Camp

Creek.) The road goes up Headwaters canyon following the thin, placid ribbon of the River of No Return toward its source. Expect good riding on gravel and dirt (or mud and puddles in June) with ankle-deep river crossings—some ridable, others, well, maybe.

Meadowlands are purple with elephanthead flowers in early summer. Past Chemekatan Campground at 3 miles from Highway 75, the road becomes more primitive and cars need high clearance. Another Salmon River crossing near the 5-mile mark halts most traffic. A jeep trail continues south 1.6 miles to Big Smoky Headwaters meadow. The headwaters of the Salmon River lie in an untrailed canyon to the southwest.

SAWTOOTH NATIONAL FOREST
Sawtooth National Recreation Area

44 FRENCHMAN CREEK

Best for: mountain biking
Opportunity for: scenic drive
11.6 miles round trip
Easy to moderate
Elevation gain: 540 feet
High point: 7,780 feet
Riding surface: dirt road
Ridable: mid-June through October
Map: USGS Frenchman Creek

Frenchman Creek canyon

Frenchman Creek canyon road is deliverance for unhurried bikers riding for relaxation, or those needing a respite from more demanding adventures. One 0.25-mile-long hill keeps this ride from being too easy. Frenchman Creek is the next drainage west of Headwaters canyon and can be linked with a descent from the Galena Wagon Road (trip 43).

From Ketchum, take Highway 75 north for 35.2 miles to the signed Frenchman Creek Road. From Stanley, go 26.5 miles on Highway 75 to the turnoff. Begin riding and stay right at the fork (go left some other time to explore a woodcutter's trail) near a stream crossing at 0.8 mile (count on wet feet in June if your pedal attack falters).

At 1.3 miles, climb a short hill, and at 1.5 miles, pass a log worm fence surrounding a forest study area. Families with children could start biking here for a level ride through the willowed canyon and its scattered beaver ponds. June through early July is a time of incredible wildflowers.

At 3.5 miles, on a short rise near the largest ponds, look back to the northeast for an unusual view of Castle Peak—18 miles away as the crow flies—rising above Pole Creek canyon in the White Clouds.

The one substantial hill starts at 4.3 miles (time for a family turnaround) and tops out at 4.6 miles, near a mining claim. At 5 miles is a boggy meadow with rutted road that will halt vehicles early in the season. At 5.6 miles, near canyon's end, pass a sheepherder's camp and perhaps a band of sheep. At 5.8 miles, the road becomes steep and rocky as it climbs to prospects high on the mountainside. Leave your bike and hike on for higher views.

SAWTOOTH NATIONAL FOREST
Sawtooth National Recreation Area

45 POLE CREEK

Best for: mountain biking
Opportunities for: scenic drive
11.1-mile loop
Easy to moderate
Elevation gain: 470 feet
High point: 7,720 feet
Riding surface: dirt and gravel roads
Ridable: June through October
Maps: USGS Alturas Lake, Horton Peak

As spring arrives, the sage and meadow country of the upper Sawtooth Valley is snow free long before higher roads and trails. An easy bike loop with some strenuous moments leads to historical Pole Creek Guard Station and up Pole Creek Road. The trip starts near the base of Galena Summit. A more adventurous beginning: descend from the summit first and sail down Galena Wagon Road described in trip 43. A Pole Creek bike loop also combines well with a ride on Valley Road to Horton Peak (trip 46).

From Ketchum, take Highway 75 for 34.7 miles north to the *first* Salmon

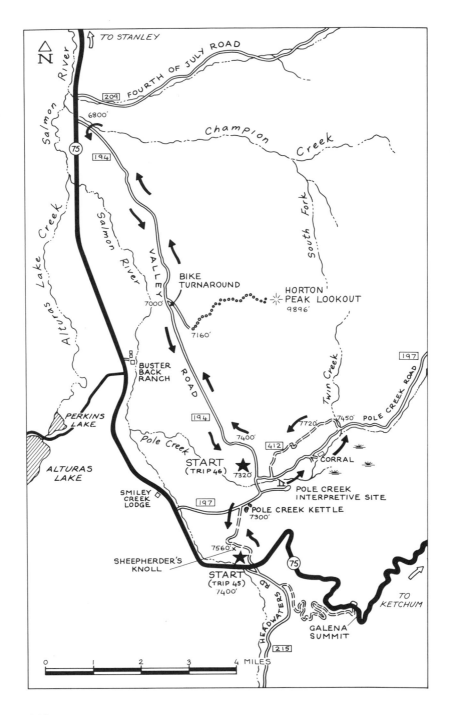

N △

TO STANLEY

FOURTH OF JULY ROAD

209

Salmon River

Champion Creek

6800'

75

194

Salmon River

Alturas Lake Creek

VALLEY

BIKE TURNAROUND

7000'

South Fork

HORTON PEAK LOOKOUT
9896'

7160'

197

ROAD

BUSTER BACK RANCH

Twin Creek

7720'   7450'   POLE CREEK ROAD

PERKINS LAKE

194

Pole Creek

7400'

412

CORRAL

ALTURAS LAKE

START
(TRIP 46) 7320' ★

POLE CREEK INTERPRETIVE SITE

SMILEY CREEK LODGE

197

POLE CREEK KETTLE
7300'

7560' x

SHEEPHERDER'S KNOLL

START
(TRIP 45)
7400' ★

HEADWATERS RD

75

TO KETCHUM

GALENA SUMMIT

215

0   1   2   3   4 MILES

River Road sign. From Stanley, drive 27.2 miles south via Highway 75. Look for a dirt, high-clearance road going north up the sagebrush hillside, on the opposite highway side from the Salmon River–Headwaters Road. Ride up a draw and at 0.5 mile, the road bends left and climbs 0.2 mile to the ridge and a circular grove of about 75 aspen trees. Later in the summer it's 75 aspens and one sheepherder's wagon—think of this as "Sheepherder's Knoll." The rugged canyon due south is Frenchman Creek. The mountain called Abe's Chair rises above Smiley Creek.

Leave the ridge and, on rutted road, coast for 0.5 mile into Pole Creek. At 1.7 miles, pass a wire gate and at 1.9 miles, join Valley Road 194. Look east in a swale for a pond known as Pole Creek Kettle, formed by the melting of an ice chunk buried in glacial drift. In May and June, nesting ducks call the kettle home, replaced by nestling cows later on.

Turn right (north) on severely corrugated Valley Road, passing at 2.4 miles a new road built in 1988 which leads a mile to the old Pole Creek Guard Station, an interpretive site. Either take this side trip now (go now if you are driving) and backtrack to Valley Road or wait a mile.

Continue on Valley Road, crossing Pole Creek by an irrigation dam at 2.7 miles, just before an intersection with Pole Creek Road 197 at 2.8 miles. Turn right (east) on Pole Creek Road. At 3.6 miles, the guard station is within quick reach 250 yards off the road across a field.

The bike loop continues up Pole Creek Road, passing a 0.5-mile-long meadow and sheep corrals, and at 5.2 miles, reaches Champion Creek trail and road 412 (not the same as Champion Lakes farther up Pole Creek). Casual bikers

Pole Creek kettle

should turn around and coast back down Pole Creek while adventurers take on overgrown and unmaintained road 412 on a 2-mile hillside workout. The trip's overall distance will be the same for either.

Road 412 begins level, then intermittently climbs the next 0.8 mile through bushes of currants and trappers tea in a clearcut. The road forks. Take the sharp left.

At 6.3 miles you're rolling downhill. Look below to Pole Creek valley and a glimpse of the ranger station. At 7.3 miles, rejoin Pole Creek Road. Retrace your route over "Sheepherder's Knoll."

SAWTOOTH NATIONAL FOREST
Sawtooth National Recreation Area

46 VALLEY ROAD, HORTON PEAK

Best for: mountain biking
Opportunities for: scenic drive, hiking
19.2 miles round trip
Easy
Elevation loss: 600 feet
High point: 7,400 feet
Riding surface: dirt, gravel, and cobble road
Ridable: mid-May through October
Maps: USGS Alturas Lake, Obsidian

Turnaround at base of Horton Peak
11.6 miles round trip
Easy
Elevation gain: 160 feet

Valley Road curves along the base of the White Cloud foothills. Mile after mile, ride with wide-angle vistas across the Sawtooth Valley to the Sawtooth peaks and glacier-carved canyons at their flanks. This trip is out-and-back so the distance can be easily shortened. A likely turnaround point is Horton Peak. A Valley Road ride also combines well with trip 45 (Pole Creek).

From Ketchum, drive Highway 75 north for 37.2 miles to a sign for Valley Road and Pole Creek Road. From Stanley, this turnoff is 24.7 miles via Highway 75. Continue 2.7 miles to a bridge and irrigation dam over Pole Creek. Park at this pleasant green oasis surrounded by sagebrush and ride 0.1 mile to a junction of Valley Road 194 and Pole Creek Road 197 where trip mileage begins. Go left (northwest) and start a slightly downhill ride.

Valley Road is now agreeable pedaling on gravel, dirt, and a small dose of river rock. A signed side road at 4.8 miles leads 1 mile to the meadows and aspen groves at the base of Horton Peak—the turnaround for a shorter trip. For a hike to Horton Peak Lookout see below.

At 6.3 miles, Valley Road enters a muddy stretch for 0.25 mile. The road here may be impassable until June. Check locally about conditions. Bikers can skirt the goo and proceed onward. As you approach Highway 75 at 9.6 miles,

Storm cloud over the Sawtooths

the road becomes rougher and rockier. The return trip will be slightly uphill and likely face afternoon winds to return to the start.

With some prior arrangements, a 17-mile one-way ride could begin at Galena Summit. Take the Galena Wagon Road (trip 43), connect to the Pole Creek loop ride (trip 45), and continue on Valley Road to Highway 75.

Side Trip: Horton Peak Lookout

      5 miles round trip
      Strenuous
      Elevation gain: 2,740 feet
      High point: 9,896 feet
      Hikable: mid-June through October
      Maps: USGS Alturas Lake, Horton Peak

Use Valley Road to reach the Horton Peak access road and go 1 mile to the base of the mountain. The trail climbs 2.5 miles, gaining 2,740 feet, to the summit's old lookout at 9,896 feet. You'll look down into Lost Creek to the north; the White Clouds to the northeast; and see (left to right) Alturas, Perkins, Pettit, and Yellow Belly lakes to the west. A short walk up the lookout trail is recommended, especially in September when the aspen trees are golden.

■ White Cloud Mountains ■

47 ROUGH CREEK, LOOKOUT MOUNTAIN

Best for: hiking
10 miles round trip
Strenuous
Elevation gain: 2,584 feet
High point: 9,984 feet
Hikable: July through October
Map: USGS Casino Lakes

Turnaround in Rough Creek Canyon
4 miles round trip
Easy
Elevation gain: 400 feet
High point: 7,800 feet

Lookout Mountain is the White Clouds candidate for the all-star lookout list. The easiest approach is from Rough Creek canyon, nearly 10 miles downriver on Highway 75 from Stanley. Cross Rough Creek bridge over the Salmon River and go 4 miles on a good-quality gravel road, suitable for passenger cars, that climbs 1,200 feet from the canyon to the trailhead.

Rough Creek is a moist, thickly wooded, wildlife-inhabited, north-facing drainage. Families can amble along the first 2 miles, admiring wildflowers and looking and listening for four-legged creatures. Besides pine squirrels you may see a slow-moving porcupine. The sandy streambed glitters with pyrite—fool's gold.

Often the path is wet and soggy, crisscrossed with rivulets. In the past, deadfall has required up-and-over scampers by hikers. But it also protects the fragile, saturated canyon trail from wheels—Rough Creek was still open to motorized use in 1989.

At 2 miles, a caved-in footbridge signals the beginning of switchbacks leading to the east ridge. At 3 miles, a sign marks the turnoff to Lookout Mountain, two more steep miles away. The main hiking trail continues southwest to Casino Lakes and Garland Lakes.

Climb toward the lookout. As you gain the ridge above Garland Creek, a trail comes in from Garland Lakes. Another 1.5 miles of ridge walking and final switchbacks brings the summit at 5 miles. And the rewards.

The Sawtooths spread across the southwestern horizon. The Salmon River

Castle Peak from Castle Divide trail

Wild White Cloud peaks from Lookout Mountain

Mountains are northwest. Prospector Peak is north and Robinson Bar Peak northeast. Trailless Rough Lake is seen at the head of Rough Creek canyon. Garland Creek and its prime elk habitat is south.

Below to the east, 20-mile-long Warm Springs canyon stretches from Born Lakes to Robinson Bar on the Salmon River. Above Warm Springs Creek is the trailless, inhospitable Swimm Lake cirque and nearby Watson Peak; in the distance gleam the famous White Cloud alabaster peaks. Lookout Mountain anchors the northeast corner of the proposed Boulder–White Cloud Wilderness.

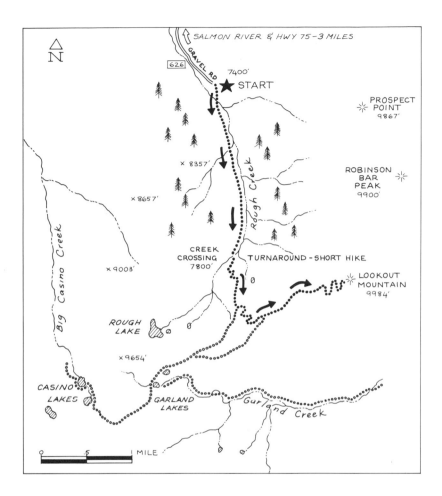

SALMON RIVER & HWY 75 – 3 MILES

626 GRAVEL RD

7400'

★ START

N

PROSPECT POINT 9867'

× 8357'

× 8657'

Rough Creek

ROBINSON BAR PEAK 9900'

Big Casino Creek

× 9003'

CREEK CROSSING 7800'

TURNAROUND – SHORT HIKE

LOOKOUT MOUNTAIN 9984'

ROUGH LAKE

× 9654'

CASINO LAKES

GARLAND LAKES

Garland Creek

0   .5   1 MILE

CHALLIS NATIONAL FOREST

48 JIMMY SMITH LAKE

Best for: hiking
Opportunities for: scenic drive
1.2 miles round trip
Easy
Elevation gain: 280 feet
High point: 6,400 feet
Hikable: year-round
Map: USGS Potaman Peak

Spring arrives early at Jimmy Smith Lake, bringing bare ground and buttercups while the Sawtooth and Wood River valleys are still deep in snow. A day-long outing to reach the East Fork Salmon River and the short walk to the frozen-over lake is a remedy for March cabin fever. Another attraction—during cold, stormy months, the East Fork is refuge for bighorn sheep, elk, and deer. From Ketchum the East Fork country is a scenic but 2-hour drive.

From Stanley, take Highway 75 down the Salmon River Canyon. Watch in winter for elk on the southern hillsides and for bald eagles near the river. At 36.5 miles, arrive at the East Fork junction. Drive up East Fork Road 120 for 14.6 miles to Jimmy Smith turnoff, passing along the way side roads for Spar Canyon, Walker Way in Road Creek (see alternative below), and scenic Herd Creek, which goes 10 miles to Herd Lake.

The Jimmy Smith dirt road goes 1.1 miles and ends, turning to a 1.1-mile trail to the lake. If the access road is muddy or blocked by snow, walk the distance. The route is usually passable. Along the steep north shore (Jimmy Smith's banks are tilted, not known for comfortable lounging) a trail leads to a finger of water in Corral Creek, a drainage beneath Potaman Peak (9,376 feet).

Jimmy Smith Lake looks like a reservoir, but the natural barrier across the

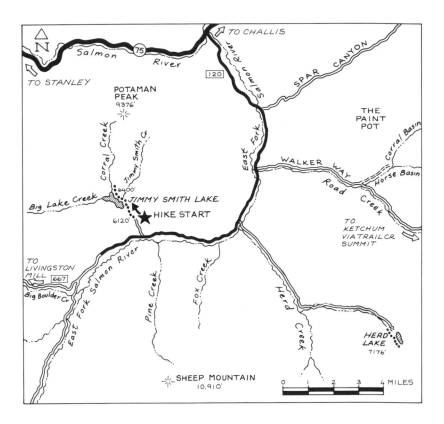

March hiking at Jimmy Smith Lake

canyon was formed by a Nebraskan ice-age mudflow down Big Lake Creek canyon millions of years ago.

Alternative Drive: Jimmy Smith Lake Road via Trail Creek and Walker Way

> 69 miles one way
> Driving surface: dirt and gravel two-wheel-drive, high-clearance road
> Drivable: May through October

From late spring onward, a trip from Ketchum to East Fork Road and Jimmy Smith Lake can go over Trail Creek Summit and Walker Way on gravel and dirt roads, rather than via Stanley. Distance is shorter, but rougher surfaces make driving time about the same (2 hours or more). Check with Lost River Ranger District in Mackay for road conditions. There are no service stations or phones along this remote route. Many travelers use the Trail Creek access to reach the East Fork and then return at day's end on the paved route via

Stanley. Such a loop has varied sights, from wide-open antelope country to the snow-covered Sawtooth Mountains.

To take Walker Way, go from Ketchum north to Sun Valley and drive Trail Creek Road for 33.8 miles to a sign for Sage Creek and Howell canyon. Go left (north). This road is called Walker Way, although intersection signs do not use that name. A Challis Forest Map is necessary to help navigate a network of dirt roads which eventually reaches the East Fork Salmon River in 28 scenic miles. At the East Fork go left (south) 7.5 miles to Jimmy Smith Lake Road.

SAWTOOTH NATIONAL FOREST
Sawtooth National Recreation Area

49 HEART LAKE, SIX LAKES BASIN

Best for: hiking
3.6 miles round trip
Moderate to difficult
Elevation gain: 560 feet
High point: 8,840 feet
Hikable: July through October
Map: USGS Washington Peak

Most hikers headed to Fourth of July Lake or deeper into the White Clouds overlook the 1-mile, primitive, unmaintained trail leading to Heart Lake and isolated Six Lakes Basin. After a confidence-building jaunt to Fourth of July and Washington lakes (trip 50), consider this hike.

In 1992 the notoriously rough Fourth of July Road was reconstructed for use by two-wheel-drive passenger cars. The old, bouldery road had long served to protect the fragile subalpine lakes in this region from overuse.

To reach Fourth of July Road, drive 46.8 miles north of Ketchum on Highway 75; from Stanley, go south on Highway 75 for 15 miles. Turn east onto the signed road. Check your odometer. Drive up the bumpy road, which improves near the foothills, cross the creek, and pass scenic picnic meadows. Soon views will be limited by forest. At about 7.9 miles, pass a bulldozed area to the left, cleared of trees (once the proposed relocation of Fourth of July trailhead).

Soon a rock mountain comes into view to the southeast. At 8.7 miles from Highway 75, look for a large turnout on the right with space for several cars. In 1992 a heart was carved into a tree marking the Heart Lake trailhead. Park and walk south, down a bank to rushing Fourth of July Creek, and hunt for a safe crossing (difficult early in the season). Heart Lake Creek enters from the south and has a well-defined footpath (not shown on 1964 Washington Peak topo) on its right side. If you don't see a distinct trail you're in the wrong drainage.

The 1-mile trail follows Heart Lake's outlet stream, skirting deadfall, charg-

One of the shallow lakes in Six Lakes Basin

ing through knee-high flower thickets, and climbing in and out of creekbed—
an interesting mile for hikers.

There's more cross-country exploring in Six Lakes Basin. Stay on Heart
Lake's east (left) side. Cross through marsh by the inlet. Above is a rockslide
with avalanche debris and mounds from mudflows. Pick your way—the going
is rough but not steep—heading toward the gap between the scree slope to the
east and the wooded ridge to the west above the lake. The first lake is more a
rock pond. Search for the other shallow lakes.

On the south ridge, Washington Peak (10,519 feet; trip 51) is nearly matched
by other summits. While rambling in the upper basin, look back at your route—
wooded knolls and clumps of forest can confuse the descent to Heart Lake.
Keep youngsters in sight, here and at Heart Lake.

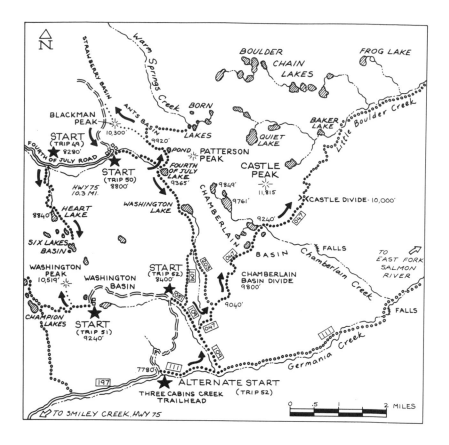

50 FOURTH OF JULY LAKE, BLACKMAN PEAK

Best for: hiking
3.2 miles round trip
Easy to moderate
Elevation gain: 525 feet
High point: 9,920 feet
Hikable: late June through October
Maps: USGS Washington Peak, Boulder Chain

The heather-edged shorelines of Fourth of July Lake and nearby Washington Lake have introduced overnight backcountry camping to generations of wilderness newcomers. Close to the lakes lies plenty of adventuring, including a scenic loop of Blackman Peak.

Reach the new trailhead, completed in 1993, via the 10-mile-long Fourth of July Road (see trip 49, Heart Lake, for directions). This road used to require high clearance and tough tires before major reconstruction was done in 1992. The old primitive and scenic trailhead at the Highland Surprise Mine has also passed into Sawtooth history.

The path to Fourth of July Lake is a brief and easy 1.6 miles with several stream crossings on footlogs and boulders. You may encounter a few motorbikes, but those times may soon be history since the region of the White Clouds has nearly unanimous support for wilderness designation.

When camping, use existing campsites; backpacking stoves are strongly recommended, as wood is scarce.

Washington Lake, a long mile to the south by signed trail, is nearly the same elevation as Fourth of July but reached by first hiking uphill, gaining 235 feet, then dropping on rocky path 200 feet. Several well-used campsites are near the outlet.

Another destination from Fourth of July Lake is north 1.3 miles to Ants Basin Divide (9,920 feet). Take the main trail from the lake's outlet a few hundred yards north to a path leading right and signed for Born Lakes. Climb sharply on eroded trail (closed to motorbikes), passing at the halfway point a small lake that's washed dust from many weary hikers. The route traverses the steep mountainside of Fourth of July canyon, skirting hulks of white bark pines, to the divide.

Ants Basin hangs on an emerald shelf above Warm Springs canyon. D. O. Lee Peak (11,342 feet) overwhelms the northeastern skyline. At the head of Warm Springs canyon to the east 1.5 miles lie much-visited Born Lakes, reached by an unofficial and often-vague trail from Ants Basin. Likewise, trail 219 from the basin into Warm Springs is obscure.

From Ants Basin Divide, it's an easy scramble to the top of Blackman Peak to the northwest; then loop back to the trailhead.

Alternative Hike: Fourth of July Lake–Blackman Peak–Strawberry Basin Loop

> 5.8 miles round trip
> Moderate to strenuous
> Elevation gain: 1,460 feet (and loss)
> High point: 10,300 feet
> Hikable: July through mid-October

Few day hikes give broader views for so few miles. For this half-day White Cloud adventure loop, bring a Washington Peak topo map and use directions given above to Fourth of July Lake and Ants Basin Divide at 2.9 miles. Go left along the blustery ridge to the base of Blackman Peak and walk 300 feet up to the top, 10,300 feet, at 3.7 miles. Enjoy a 360-degree view of the white Cloud world, including Castle Peak to the east and distant Sawtooths and Stanley Basin to the west.

For a loop, descend the steep north slope on goat paths, staying away from the precipitous drop-off and pinnacles on the peak's east face, to a mining trail into Ants Basin at 4.2 miles. Continue north and hike cross-country up the ridge to look north into Strawberry Basin at 4.3 miles. Below, a mining road cuts across the mountainside and alpine meadows to the Silver Dollar Mine. Retrace your steps off the ridge and go west over a gentle hillside to meet the road before it drops into the basin.

Follow it left (south) as it traverses below Blackman Peak back to Fourth of July trailhead at 5.8 miles. (This mining road is closed to motorized travel except by owners of claims in the Strawberry Basin area).

An ascent of Blackman Peak is easy enough for novice hikers and gives good practice in routefinding and map reading in wide-open terrain. However, be wary of thunderstorms, and cancel your high-ridge wanders if clouds threaten.

Ridge walking near Fourth of July Lake

51 WASHINGTON PEAK

Best for: hiking and scrambling
Opportunities for: scenic drive
2.6 miles round trip
Moderate to strenuous
Elevation gain: 1,279 feet
High point: 10,519 feet
Hikable: July through October
Maps: USGS Washington Peak, Horton Peak

Washington Peak (10,519 feet) is the highest point (by 5 feet) on an S-shaped ridge curving 5 miles in the southwestern White Clouds. The wind-blown summit is a mild walk-up, manageable by average hikers who are otherwise wary of heights. A little trembling will come in thunderstorms, or from the final 4 miles of access road to Washington Basin where the climb begins. For non-scramblers there's plentiful low-altitude exploring about the basin.

Start early for the long drive to the basin. The high-clearance road is sometimes rough and steep; four-wheel drive is helpful. From Ketchum, take Highway 75 north over Galena Summit 36 miles to graveled Valley Road 194. From Stanley, go 25 miles south via Highway 75 to the turnoff. From this point Washington Basin is 16.5 miles away—1.5 hours of driving time.

Go north on Valley Road for 2.7 miles to a junction for Pole Creek Road 197 and turn right. Pass by Grand Prize trailhead at 6.6 miles. The road narrows and roughens, passing Pole Creek Summit (8,400 feet) at 9.5 miles.

Past the summit, descend into Germania Creek. At 10.5 miles pass Champion Lakes trailhead (a 1-mile hike upward leads to the ridge overlooking the lakes a mile below). The road improves as it drops to a ford of Germania Creek (a potential hazard early in the season) just before Three Cabins trailhead at 12.5 miles. Turn left on the Washington Basin jeep trail.

Half a mile beyond Three Cabins, scrape across a ravine at a hairpin corner. The road climbs, improves, and drops to Washington Creek at 14.5 miles. A steep, mean mile lies ahead. When Croesus Peak comes into view, the basin is at hand.

Once the road levels out in the basin by an old cabin, continue another 0.7 mile to a pond and rusting boiler. Park by the boiler and walk the final 0.2 mile of road, stretching legs for the climb ahead. As you pass two decrepit cabins, watch right for a trail going west with a sign for Champion Lakes. (Be sure you're on the correct route. Another path requiring scrambles on all fours goes over the southern saddle to Germania Basin or up Croesus Peak—a different adventure. Traversing from the south saddle to Champion Lakes trail is mighty tedious.)

Climb a gravelly 0.5 mile, gaining 800 feet, to the basin rim and look upon Champion Lakes. Washington Peak is north, along the scree ridgeline, another 0.6 mile farther and 479 feet higher. At the summit, Six Lakes Basin and Heart Lake are below to the north. The cream-colored mountain of D. O. Lee Peak rises to the northeast; Castle Peak is east. The 'tooths are west, the Boulders south. For Sawtooth Country travelers it's a geography test at 10,519 feet.

Scanning the route to Washington Peak

52 CASTLE DIVIDE, CASTLE PEAK

Best for: hiking
15.0 miles round trip
Strenuous
Elevation gain: 3,280 feet
High point: 10,000 feet
Hikable: July through mid-October
Maps: USGS Boulder Chain Lakes, Galena Peak,
   Washington Peak, Horton Peak

Turnaround 1: Chamberlain Basin Divide
8.4 miles round trip
Strenuous
Elevation gain: 1,880 feet
High point: 9,800 feet

Turnaround 2: Chamberlain Basin
11.2 miles round trip
Strenuous
Elevation gain: 2,480 feet
High point: 9,800 feet

For an up-close look at Castle Peak (11,815 feet), begin early on a long summer day. The drive to the trailhead is long and slow. Be trail-toughened from other hikes; the elevation gain is substantial. Major trail reconstruction in 1994 made the scenic trek less steep but longer.

Follow access directions in trip 51 (Washington Peak) to Three Cabins Creek trailhead in Germania Creek. A high-clearance vehicle is needed.

At Three Cabins, continue on the Washington Basin jeep road. The gully-washed, hairpin turn 0.5 mile up is the worst impediment, then the road improves. (If your vehicle gives up at the hairpin, go back to Three Cabins trailhead and begin the hike using Germania Creek Trail 111. Take trail 111 for 1.3 miles, cross Washington Lake Creek by log, and watch closely in 0.25 mile for trail 109 angling left [the sign may be missing]. Trail 109 climbs steeply 1 mile to join trail 047. Starting at Three Cabins adds 3 miles round trip and 480 feet change in elevation to the hike.)

At 2.5 miles, the road crosses Washington Creek. Just after the ford, look for trail 051 entering from the wooded hillside to the right (east). There is a registration box in the trees.

From the Washington Basin road, take trail 051 across a small creek to a grassy hillside. At 0.2 mile, trail 109 coming from Washington Lake Creek joins in (shown on Forest Service maps but not on the 1967 Boulder Chain Lakes topo). Continue following Washington Lake Creek (now on trail 109) downhill and cross it at 1 mile. Immediately turn left, uphill, on signed trail 047.

This is a key turn—don't miss it on the return trip. A right turn leads to Germania Creek 1 mile below and back 1.5 miles to Three Cabins.

Next begin a 3-mile upward trek, gaining 1,640 feet to the divide. At rest stops, look south across Germania Creek canyon to Deer Creek, MacRae Creek, and Alta Creek in the Boulder Mountains. After 1.3 mile of climbing, trail 203 from Washington Lake and Fourth of July Lake intersects your route. For years, a vintage sign, gnawed in winter by porcupines, has greeted weary hikers here. It's another 1.7-mile assault to Chamberlain Basin Divide (9,600 feet) at 4.2 miles. The divide makes a good turnaround point for an 8.4-mile round-trip day hike.

From the divide, look across the expanse of Chamberlain Basin to the breadth (2.5 miles) of Castle Peak's southern face. A network of scree chutes criss-crosses two-thirds of the mountain, and canyons of sand spill from the right flank. Goats graze among the stunted growth of the krummholz.

From the divide, drop 600 feet to the basin and head for Castle Peak. Pass a small lake and reach at 5.6 miles the largest Chamberlain Lake at Castle Peak's base. More lakes lie a mile northwest, reached by path along the inlet stream. The distractions are many—watch the time. And make plans to return with a backpack and explore further. You may explore Chamberlain Basin and return—a round trip of 11.2 miles.

Castle Divide (10,000 feet) is 2 miles farther and 800 feet up from the basin. The White Clouds have many spectacular settings; Castle Divide is among them. Castle Peak's east face looms above the divide. In the early 1970s an open pit mine was planned to be carved from that face. This industrial abomination was averted, thanks to efforts of environmentalists. Five miles away at Baker Lake, the mining camp left from that tumultuous period has largely been hauled away with only scattered mining wreckage left in the White Cloud wildlands.

While on the divide, look for goats—unless it's post-Labor Day, when hunting season has them hiding. Turn east for views of the long ridges above Little Boulder, Wickiup, and Chamberlain Creek canyons—drainages leading to the East Fork of the Salmon River.

Descending a talus chute near Ants Basin Divide in the
White Cloud Mountains

■Galena to Pioneer Mountains■

Smoky Mountains

SAWTOOTH NATIONAL FOREST
Sawtooth National Recreation Area

53 BAKER CREEK AND PRAIRIE CREEK LAKES

Best for: hiking
Opportunities for: scenic drive
4.0 miles to 10 miles round trip; 10.8-mile loop
Easy to moderate
Elevation gain: 880 to 1,570 feet
High point: 8,870 feet
Hikable: mid-June through October
Map: USGS Galena

A group of Smoky Mountain lakes in Baker Creek and Prairie Creek canyons near Ketchum are among the most recommended close-to-town hikes. For solitude, go on weekdays or venture onward from these popular lakes. Much of Idaho's great Smoky Mountains is more than a day hike away.

There's a preferred order for novice hikers or youngsters to visit the five lakes. Start with Baker Lake. The short distance makes it an easy choice, and upper Baker Creek canyon offers alpine views. Next comes Mill Lake: fishless, but more of a backcountry experience than the grooved, dusty path to Baker. Third in line is Norton Lakes: farther, but more handsome.

The order of the final two, Prairie and Miner lakes, is a toss-up. The trail to Miner is shorter but steeper; the Prairie Lakes have more exploring nearby and a milder climb, but the entire route is open (as of 1989) to motorbikes. It's possible to see both Prairie Lakes and Miner Lake in one scenic trip using a link trail.

Baker Creek and Prairie Creek are both reached on Highway 75 north of Ketchum—15.4 miles to Baker Creek Road 162 and 18.6 miles to Prairie Creek Road 179. The distances from Stanley are 43.2 miles to Prairie Creek, 46.4 miles to Baker Creek.

Baker Lake

4.0 miles round trip
Easy to moderate
Elevation gain: 880 feet
High point: 8,796 feet

Baker Lake

Drive to the end of Baker Creek Road, where the trail begins. In 1994 the old steep, eroded path was reconstructed and rerouted, adding about 1.5 miles round trip to the hike. From the registration box, step on rocks across the shallow side stream which flows from the lake. Meander up the sagebrush-covered hillside. Before you enter the woods on the ridge, look across the wide, rugged upper canyon to Baker Peak rising 10,174 feet (reachable by cross-country hiking and an easy scramble). Continue through forest to the lake. Baker Lake is small, but deep, and serves as a brood lake for California golden trout. Check fishing regulations (currently, catch-and-release rules are in force; use artificial flies or lures with a single, barbless hook).

Norton Lakes in Baker Creek Canyon
　　　　5 miles round trip (to first lake)
　　　　Moderate
　　　　Elevation gain: 1,360 feet
　　　　High point: 8,960 feet

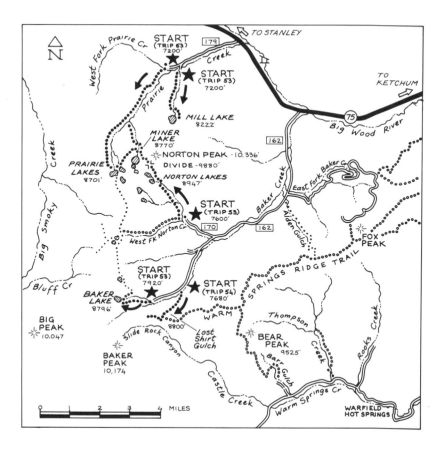

Rainy day in Idaho's Smoky Mountains

Go 6 miles up Baker Creek Road, turn right on Norton Creek Road 170, and drive 1.3 miles to the trailhead by Norton Creek's eroded banks. Scan the high rocks for a white spot—perhaps a browsing nanny goat. Cross the eroded stream on rocks. Take the Norton Lake path past the trail register and climb up the canyon, gaining a noticeable 1,360 feet to the lake at 2.5 miles. Indifferent trout swim close to shore (fishing *can* be excellent).

Upper Norton Lake is just 0.3 mile away by path. From the upper lake it's another mile to the Norton Lake–Miner Lake divide (9,880 feet). Miner Lake is seen below. Norton Peak (10,335 feet) is reached by experienced scramblers from the saddle.

Mill Lake

> 4.4 miles round trip
> Easy to moderate
> Elevation gain: 1,120 feet
> High point: 8,280 feet

Take Prairie Creek road 2.2 miles and watch for a side road going left with a sign for Mill Lake. Park by the stream at a large campsite and look for a dry footlog (or step in for a chilly wade; bring wading shoes if you like). June's deep water may require you to postpone your hike. Walk up a dirt wood-cutting road, which soon turns to trail and hops Mill Creek on a soggy bridge.

After a pleasant stretch above Mill Creek, where snow from avalanches may linger into June, cross the stream again at 1 mile and climb steadily to the ridge just above the lake. This is the trip's highest point, with views of Prairie Creek canyon and the Boulder Mountains. Barren Mill Lake is large but shallow. Kids can safely explore the shoreline, and there's another mile of canyon for more primitive adventuring.

Prairie Lakes

> 10 miles round trip
> Moderate
> Elevation gain: 1,500 feet
> High point: 8,701 feet

To reach Prairie Lakes or Miner Lake, take Prairie Creek Road 2.5 miles to its end, and park. Cross the West Fork of Prairie Creek on a hefty log. After 2.5 wooded miles the trail forks. Stay right for Prairie Lakes (left goes to Miner Lake in Miner canyon). The Prairie Lakes route continues climbing, crossing many rock and log waterbars and an eroded section of sand and gravel (why mountain bikers are seldom seen here). Watch for goats near timberline and along the ravines and outcroppings to the west. At 4.8 miles, reach the largest lake (elevation 8,701 feet). A sign points left for Miner Lake. Follow it 0.2 mile and, through the trees, look for two smaller and more pristine lakes. Prairie Lakes trail is currently open to motorbikes.

Miner Lake

> 8.4 miles round trip
> Moderate
> Elevation gain: 1,570 feet
> High point: 8,870 feet

Use the same trail access as for Prairie Lake, but go left at the signed fork at 2.5 miles and down to a crossing of Prairie Creek on rocks or logs. Shortly, cross the stream again. Both crossings are difficult until spring runoff subsides in mid-June or later. The next section of trail is steep and eroded as it climbs toward the ridge. Miner Creek spills through the ravine to the left. At 3.4 miles, reach an easy creek crossing and continue to the lake at 4.2 miles. Miner Lake is snug in an alpine pocket of scree and bluffs. Look for goats. Limited camping is along the overused south shore. A trail zigzags over the southwestern mountainside to Norton Lakes.

Prairie Lake–Miner Lake Loop

> 10.8 miles
> Moderate
> Elevation gain: 1,640 feet
> High point: 8,870 feet

This loop is the way to see Prairie and Miner lakes. The varied, lofty views are worth the extra distance. Go to Prairie Lake and take the signed path going left to Miner Lake. The link trail traverses the mountainside between Prairie canyon and Miner canyon and provides a seldom-seen view into the hidden highlands across Prairie Creek to the west. Tie into the Miner Lake trail just below the lake. Go right, climbing 0.2 mile to Miner Lake at 5.4 miles. Return via Miner canyon to the trailhead.

In June and early July, first check out the ford of Prairie Creek near the Prairie–Miner junction. If the water is too deep, plan your loop hike for a later time.

SAWTOOTH NATIONAL FOREST

54 LOST SHIRT GULCH

Best for: hiking
3 miles round trip
Moderate to strenuous
Elevation gain: 1,120 feet
High point: 8,800 feet
Hikable: June through October
Map: USGS Baker Peak

Baker Peak at the head of Slide Rock canyon

A sterling view of Baker Peak and Slide Rock canyon awaits hikers who find Lost Shirt Gulch and climb the short, steep trail to Lost Shirt ridge.

From Ketchum, drive 15.4 miles north to Baker Creek Road 162 (or from Stanley, 46.4 miles south) and go 8.5 miles to a sign for Lost Shirt Gulch and a primitive road going left (south) to a campsite. Park and cross Baker Creek by logs, rocks, or wading. Go south across a clearing 100 yards toward a dry streambed and walk up the right side. Look for blazes on the pines.

Within 300 yards of the road the trail becomes well defined. The rocky path follows bluebell-lined Lost Shirt Creek, crossing it several times before staying on the right side (west) and climbing the timbered and grassy slope toward the ridge. Some sections are eroded and hard work. Rest and look back at Baker Creek canyon and north to the Boulders.

At 1.3 miles, reach the forested crest and old signs for Baker Peak, Castle Creek, and Warm Springs Ridge. Go right, on a dim path, upward 0.25 mile onto the sage-covered hillside. Expansive Baker Peak overpowers the western skyline—an alpine zone of tundra, krummholz, and snowmelt cascades. Slide Rock Creek spills from the northeast face and, after a mile, becomes known as Castle Creek (named for Castle Rock on Warm Springs Road west of Ketchum). The upper Castle Creek trail shown on maps no longer exists. Listen for coyotes. Watch for elk in the meadows.

SAWTOOTH NATIONAL FOREST

55 KETCHUM FAT-TIRE CLASSIC: *ADAMS GULCH*

Best for: mountain biking
Opportunities for: hiking
Up to 7.6 miles round trip
Easy
Elevation gain: 200 to 600 feet
High point: 6,600 feet
Riding surface: dirt road and trails
Ridable: May through October
Map: USGS Griffin Butte

Anticipating a wet-footed, mud-dotted biking adventure in Adams Gulch is reason why Sun Valley vacationers pack old tennis shoes and extra pedaling clothes. There are nine stream crossings (and that's only one-way) on Adams Gulch Road. Rustic footbridges are in place, so getting splattered is optional, but the wheeled brigades that daily ride the gulch covet the rocky creek fords. For biking newcomers, the gentle Adams Gulch road is—a good place to get your feet wet.

In addition, there's more adventurous riding on two hillside trails—Shady Side goes through lodgepole pines; Adams Gulch Loop goes through aspen trees. A network of other, more difficult routes with steeper ascents, including

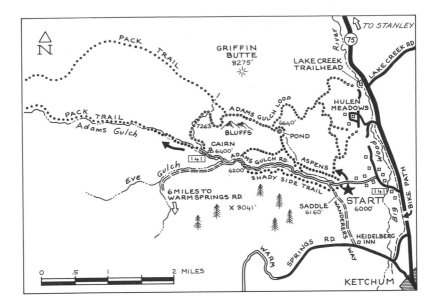

the recently added Lane's Trail, are nearby, but the short rides here focus on mellow terrain.

To reach Adams Gulch go from Ketchum's Main Street stoplight for 1.5 miles north on Highway 75 to Adams Gulch Road 141 and turn left. Go downhill, crossing the Big Wood River, and follow the signed road to the right (north). A quarter mile past the Big Wood River bridge the road bends left, uphill, and passes through a pole archway with a Private Property sign. Continue on the road, which is available for public access to the National Forest boundary and trailhead parking just ahead to the left. Both are about 1 mile from Highway 75. (You can also reach road 141 by taking the bike path north from Ketchum.)

Adams Gulch Road

 7.6 miles round trip
 Easy
 Elevation gain: 600 feet
 High point: 6,600 feet

For the easiest gulch ride, leave the trailhead parking lot and follow dirt Adams Gulch Road 141 up the main canyon. Although locally considered a breeze of a trip, you'll notice the effort of fat-tire pedaling on a slight upgrade at 6,000 feet elevation. Almost immediately, the first stream crossing is faced. Either walk your bike across the two-log footbridge or choose a line through the creekbed cobbles (this ford may be bone dry in August). Eight more crossings lie ahead—all are ridable in low water.

Family outing in Adams Gulch

In May and June, wildflowers color the canyon, and in all months, red-tailed hawks drift above the bluffs to the north. At 2.2 miles from the trailhead and after five watery crossings, pass a sign for Eves Gulch and the West Fork of Warm Springs on the left (difficult biking). At 2.7 miles and three more fords, bypass a rock cairn on the right which marks the turnoff for the western-most link of the Adams Gulch Loop trail. (The loop trail ascends to the ridge, traverses above the bluffs, and connects in over 4 miles back to Adams Gulch Road—a challenging, scenic route for agile bikers.)

The cairn is often the turnaround for briefer round-trip rides, although the wooded road continues for another 0.5 mile and again crosses Adams Gulch Creek. If you ride farther up the road, take the packtrail going right at 3 miles, just before a log fence. At 3.8 miles, the path becomes overly rugged—time to coast back.

Aspen Loop Ride
2 miles
Easy
Elevation gain: 200 feet
High point: 6,200 feet

Across from the trailhead, before the first stream crossing, take a path going right (north). In 100 yards at a Y, stay left on the Adams Gulch Loop trail. Pedal upward through sage and enter a stand of aspens—magnificent in autumn gold, or when crisp autumn leaves are hub-high. At 0.8 mile, pass a side trail descending left 0.1 mile to the creek and Adams Gulch Road (a shortcut that avoids the upcoming hill). Keep straight, walking your bike up a sharp incline and at 0.9 mile, come to a Y junction of the loop trail. Go left (see side trip to pond, below), downhill to meet Adams Gulch Road at 1 mile and coast a mile back to the start.

Shady Side Loop
> 3.5 miles
> Easy
> Elevation gain: 200 feet
> High point: 6,200 feet

To reach Shady Side, leave the trailhead and ride up the road to the third stream crossing at 1.7 miles and nearby signed Shady Side on the left (south). Shady Side's 1.5-mile length was built mostly by volunteers in 1988. It weaves through the pines on the hillside, and at 3.2 miles, it meets an old jeep road going over the saddle to Warm Springs. Go left and rejoin Adams Gulch Road and return to the trailhead at 3.5 miles. A loop of Shady Side and the aspen section of Adams Gulch Loop is also a 3.5-mile ride.

(From Adams Gulch Road to Warm Springs Road via Wanderers Way just past the Heidleberg Inn is 1 mile—an alternative route back to Ketchum.)

Side Trip to Pond
> 1.8 miles round trip
> Easy to moderate for hiking, difficult for biking
> Elevation gain: 800 feet (and loss)
> High point: 6,800 feet

Take the Aspen Loop described above and at the 0.9-mile junction, go right up the draw for 0.6 mile to a small woodland pond. Go another 0.3 mile to crest the ridge and see the Pioneer Mountains to the east. This is the favorite footpath in the gulch, and after pushing your bike its length, you may choose next time to hike rather than bike.

The Adams Gulch trail system also ties into the well-signed Lake Creek National Recreation Trail network farther north. The Ketchum Ranger District provides a Lake Creek–Adams Gulch trail brochure. In 1995, mountain bikes were still permitted on the Lake Creek system, but a review and perhaps some restrictions may be forthcoming. Lake Creek receives heavy use by hikers and runners and is reachable by paved bike path from Ketchum.

Boulder Mountains

56 NORTH FORK BIG WOOD RIVER HIKES

Best for: hiking
Moderate
Hikable: June through October, unless noted
Map: USGS Amber Lakes

North Fork canyon of the Big Wood River is a backyard wilderness for Hailey, Ketchum, and Sun Valley residents on short flights from their towns. The North Fork is nearly lakeless, but there are compensations: short or long walks amid cloud-capped ridges soaring to 11,000 feet; beguiling avalanche lessons from those ridges; deer and elk, owls and warblers; and flowers—even in dry August—thriving in mossy springs and crevices.

Access is just 8 miles north of Ketchum on Highway 75 to North Fork Road 146 by the SNRA headquarters. From Stanley, take Highway 75 southeast for 53.7 miles. Passenger cars can handle the 5-mile North Fork Road; it's a "Sunday drive" favorite. North Fork canyon is lined in summer with happy campers alternately warming lawnchairs and baiting trout hooks. For bicyclists the 5-mile gravel and broken shale North Fork Road is washboard-type riding, at least until Cougar Campground at 3.5 miles, where it becomes more primitive and smoother pedaling.

For hikers there are four drainages to explore: Murdock Creek, East Fork of the North Fork, West Fork of the North Fork, and, simply, the North Fork. The most visited destination is the main stem, followed by the West Fork. Trails are rougher and seldom maintained in Murdock Creek and the East Fork. Most of the North Fork region has been recommended by the Sawtooth Forest as part of the proposed Boulder–White Cloud Wilderness.

Murdock Creek

6 miles round trip
Moderate
Elevation gain: 1,000 feet
High point: 7,400 feet

A 3-mile-long trail climbs moderately up the North Fork's first side canyon. After the first mile, Murdock Creek receives little use so there's a chance for solitude. Drive up North Fork Road for 1.2 miles and turn right at Murdock Creek. Pass sheep corrals and park where the road is blocked off at 0.4 mile. Cross Murdock Creek on logs or rocks. Follow an old logging road which becomes a trail in 0.5 mile and offers more palatable hiking. At 1 mile, cross the creek on a skinny log. Shortly, the path climbs steeply above an eroding bank. There are more precipitous, sloughing sections ahead. It's passable to hikers, but narrow for horses—you'll rarely see riders here.

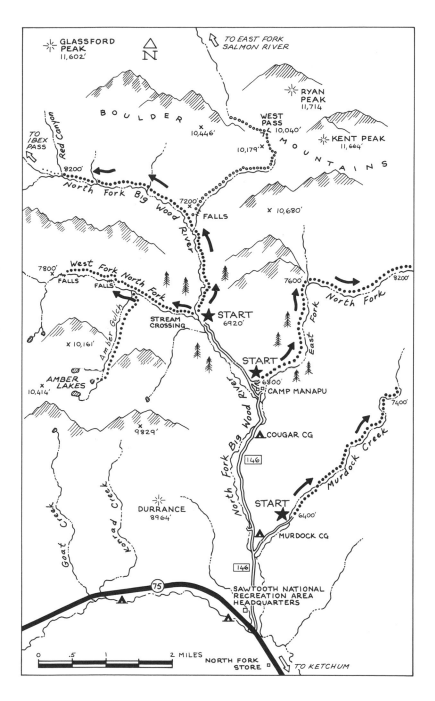

GLASSFORD PEAK 11,602'

TO EAST FORK SALMON RIVER

N

RYAN PEAK 11,714'

BOULDER

WEST PASS 10,040'

x 10,446'

KENT PEAK 11,664'

10,179' x

MOUNTAINS

TO IBEX PASS

Red Canyon

8200'

North Fork Big Wood River

7200' x

FALLS

x 10,680'

West Fork North Fork

7800'

FALLS

FALLS

7600'

North Fork

8200'

Amber Gulch

STREAM CROSSING

START 6920'

East Fork

x 10,161'

START 6800'

CAMP MANAPU

AMBER LAKES x 10,414'

7400'

x 9829'

COUGAR CG

Murdock Creek

North Fork Big Wood River

146

Goat Creek

Konrad Creek

DURRANCE 8964'

START 6400'

MURDOCK CG

146

SAWTOOTH NATIONAL RECREATION AREA HEADQUARTERS

75

0   .5   1   2 MILES

NORTH FORK STORE

TO KETCHUM

For the next 2 miles the trail traverses the hillsides through sage, forest, and talus above the willows and undergrowth flourishing along the stream. Wildflowers line the path and so do stinging nettle, especially in the second mile. (In May and June nettles are too short to bother; by August, grazing sheep will have helped tromp them down.)

Twin waterfalls, East Fork of the North Fork Big Wood River

Ahead to the east rises the 10,500-foot headwall of Murdock Creek canyon; southward are ominous avalanche chutes. At trail's end at 3 miles, three drainages merge in a tangle of slide-swept slopes.

East Fork

> 8 miles round trip
> Moderate
> Elevation gain: 1,400 feet
> High point: 8,200 feet
> Map: USGS Rock Roll Canyon (optional)

The second side canyon of the North Fork lies beneath Kent Peak's southern flank. The East Fork is a drainage fraught with avalanches, but few visitors. The 4-mile trail receives much of its use by horsemen during fall hunting season. For hikers June is the best month. The East Fork River cascades below the trail and wildflowers brighten the talus slopes.

Drive up North Fork Road for 4 miles, passing Camp Manapu, to a sign for East Fork trail. Turn right and drive 0.2 mile, parking before a steep, rutted pitch. Walk along the road 0.2 mile and pick up the trail, which traverses through open forest above the stream. Across the valley, slide chutes spew trees to the creek. After an upward mile the path crosses rockslides bedecked with maple and currants. In 2 miles cross a side stream from a turbulent canyon dividing Kent Peak and the unnamed pyramidal peak (10,680 feet).

Downed trees surround the path as it goes another 0.5 mile to a large clearing where the East Fork braids through a willow flat. From this point the way becomes indistinct. Beyond the East Fork headwall lie the remote upper breaks of Trail Creek. Portions of trail there shown on maps have vanished.

West Fork

> 7 miles round trip
> Moderate
> Elevation gain: 880 feet
> High point: 7,800 feet

From the SNRA headquarters it's 5.2 miles to road's end and the start of both the West Fork and the North Fork trails. Signs point across the flood plain to the West Fork trail and registration box which are out of sight from the parking area.

To cross the creek, use an upstream footlog (unless it's washed away; then wade if water level permits). There are no more crossings despite false paths or the route shown on the 1967 Amber Lakes topo. Begin a moderate ascent through forest, and at 1 mile, reach a side path toward Amber Gulch, the avalanche-strewn drainage to the west. (Trail work in 1994 reconstructed some of the steep Amber Lakes path which gains 2,000 feet in 3.3 miles to a small pond in the basin below the two Amber Lakes. A topo map is helpful to find the lakes from the end of the constructed trail.)

Past Amber Gulch, the West Fork trail, faint at times, continues climbing gently, staying on the right side of the stream. To the southwest rises the ridge separating West Fork from Boulder Basin mines. At 3.5 miles, the maintained trail fades near a moss-walled chasm where the cascading creek mists the red and yellow petals of Sitka columbine.

North Fork

> 9 miles round trip
> Moderate
> Elevation gain: 1,280 feet
> High point: 8,200 feet

A half-mile walk here brings views of 11,000-foot rugged ridges and the scenery never lessens. Drive to the end of the North Fork Road, as above. Take the right path uphill, passing the registration box and gaining 80 feet to reach a wooded ridge where violets grow in the shade. The path then turns downhill to the stream. The hiker trail stays right, traversing a gravelly, sloughing bank above the North Fork where steps need to be anchored firmly (resort to all fours if necessary). Frequently a snowslide fills the creek below.

After the traverse, the path fades in grass but reappears as it heads for a stand of old-growth timber. Look for woodpeckers and owls in the aging Douglas firs and for bright-colored warblers in the nearby willows. The canyon becomes more rugged, displaying spraying waterfalls and craggy ravines, bent trees blasted by snow, and unending springs with bog orchids, monkshood, and cinquefoil. Watch for stinging nettle in overgrown sections.

At 1.25 miles cross a bouldery stream. At 1.5 miles in a grassy clearing, cairns may mark the easily-missed turnoff for wild West Pass, 10,040 feet high, and 2 miles away, on the roof of the Boulder Mountains. Past the West Pass junction, the main North Fork canyon path continues to climb. At 4.5 miles, the trail disappears and ends in thick woods where a sheepherder has carved "Juan Balboa, 17th of July 1965" into a rough-hewn log table. Hiking onward is difficult; three drainages merge, and seasoned scramblers face mouthwatering choices. To the north lies a canyon of reddish scree and cliffs. The center (northwest) canyon has a vague path that disappears before reaching Ibex Pass, 2,000 feet above (named for the Old World goat).

CHALLIS NATIONAL FOREST

57 HUNTER CREEK SUMMIT

> Best for: hiking
> Opportunities for: scenic drive, mountain biking
> 5 miles round trip
> Moderate
> Elevation gain: 1,280 feet
> High point: 9,400 feet
> Hikable: late June through October
> Maps: USGS Meridian Peak, Ryan Peak

Hunter Creek lies in a far-flung corner of the Boulder Mountains that's advocated by Idaho conservationists for wilderness designation. One trip to the summit leads to others in the eastern Boulder–White Clouds area. There aren't many lakes. The region appeals to experienced hikers wanting to go where trails are undusted, where there are no trails.

From Ketchum, drive to Sun Valley and continue on Trail Creek Road 408 for 20 miles to the North Fork Big Lost River Road 128. Turn left. North Fork canyon begins in sage and rimrock and evolves to wooded north-facing slopes and alpine ridges over 11,000 feet. More than a dozen side canyons join the main drainage. Moose have been introduced to the willow-covered valley floor.

Drive up the North Fork for 12.6 miles (ignoring a side road going left at Bear Creek) and gaining 1,000 feet to road's end at Hunter Creek trail.   The

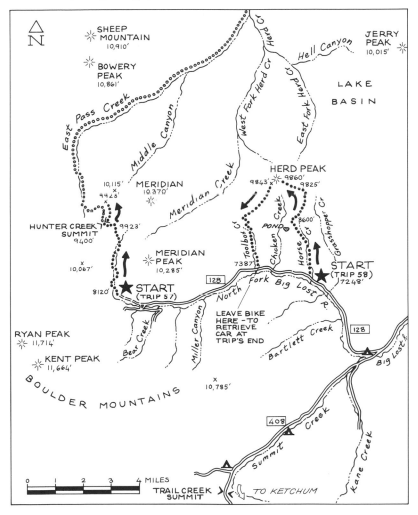

Bowery Peak near Hunter Creek Summit trail

last 1.5 miles are high-clearance, and soft meadows may be impassable early in the season. For mountain bikers the road is fair riding—some parts are badly washboarded.

From the road's end the Boulder Mountain skyline shows Kent Peak to the left, the eastern bulwark of Ryan Peak to the right.

The trail to Hunter Creek Summit begins up a steep hill, just past a Closed to Motor Vehicles sign, and then goes through woodlands along the stream which is crossed several times by rocks or logs. At 1.8 miles, leave the creek bottom and start ascending the ridge, gaining 880 feet in the next 0.7 mile. At 2.5 miles the trail tops out in a clearing at Hunter Creek Summit (9,400 feet).

For the views you came for, go right, on a path up the windswept ridge, leaving the main trail (which descends northwest into East Pass Creek and eventually reaches the East Fork Salmon River).

Follow the ridge path upward for several hundred yards and find a comfortable vantage point among the stunted pines and miniature alpine flowers—or keep going 0.8 mile to a knob at 9,923 feet. Look south to the Pioneer Range and southwest to green, tundra goat pastures on the Boulders. North is the craggy east face of Bowery Peak.

58 HERD PEAK

Best for: hiking
10 miles one way
Difficult
Elevation gain: 2,612 feet, loss 2,473 feet
High point: 9,860 feet
Hikable: mid-May through October
Maps: USGS Herd Peak, plus optional maps: Herd Lake,
    Meridian Peak, Bowery Peak, Harry Canyon

Before a Herd Peak visit, first go to Hunter Creek Summit (trip 57) for an easy introduction to the Boulder–White Clouds eastern ecosystem. A Herd Peak loop is a more demanding trip, best for experienced hikers seeking a remote outing and skilled in map reading. Topos of this high, dry region show mostly white, signifying a land of grass, sage, and rimrock. But northern slopes are thickly timbered, and elk roam here, as well as antelope. Try this Herd Peak adventure in June.

Start early. You'll need a full day and clear weather free of thunderstorms. Bring plenty of water and the Herd Peak topo (not Herd Lake). Some trail sections are faint, junctions are unsigned, and the vast terrain is mostly un-visited except by fall hunters. In other words, it's magnificent country and recommended strongly by conservationists for wilderness designation. You'll also need to leave a bicycle at trip's end, in order to retrieve your car a few miles away.

From Ketchum, drive to Sun Valley and take scenic and car-battering Trail Creek Road 408 over Trail Creek Summit for 20 miles to the North Fork of the Big Lost River Road 128 going left (north). Both roads are drivable in a family sedan, and you may see moose walking up Trail Creek Road. Go up the North Fork 4.3 miles to a sign for Horse Creek—the departure point. But travel 2.1 miles farther up the road and leave the bike at Toolbox Creek (hide it from view in Toolbox canyon). Return to Horse Creek and park.

The topo shows a jeep road in Horse Creek, but only cow trails go up the canyon. In June you should miss the herd and maybe see moose, elk, and antelope instead. Pick a path, eventually staying left of the creek, and after 1.8 miles, arrive at a large flat. Go straight (northwest), following the stream which ends as you climb through sage (and possibly snow) to gain an 8,600-foot saddle above Chicken Creek.

From the saddle, view the arduous route ahead: a circling of Chicken Creek on the treeless, skyline ridge. A trail goes right, northeast, sharply up the saddle, and disappears before reaching knoll 9,312—a breathless gain of over 700 feet in 0.5 mile. Another 200-foot climb and you're overlooking Grasshopper Creek to the east. Continue up the barren ridge to reach, at 5 miles from North Fork Road, wind-scoured knoll 9,825. For the first time you see the high rolling prairies, plateaus, and canyons of the eastern White Clouds.

Descent from Herd Peak ridge, Boulder Mountains in the distance

Below is the East Fork of Herd Creek; the proposed BLM Wilderness of Jerry Peak is northeast. Far east is the Lost River Range, southward Devil's Bedstead rises in the Pioneers, and Peak 10,785 towers over Miller canyon in the Boulders.

Herd Peak is within easy reach, over a mile distant to the west on what is now an obvious trail. A geological marker on a rock outcropping, just a few yards higher than the trail, identifies Herd Peak's inconspicuous summit.

From Herd Peak the trail goes between two rocky knolls and descends a gradual 0.5 mile through sage to a saddle dividing Meridian Creek and Chicken Creek, about 7 miles into the trip. If snowdrifts linger and obscure the trail, search until you relocate its well-defined tread. The next mile is potentially confusing, the path varies from the route on the 1967 topo map, and the pack-trail is your easiest ticket home.

The path heads south from the saddle, then turns west, skirting a tributary of Meridian Creek, and reaches the top of timbered Toolbox Creek. Unsigned side paths split for Meridian Peak and Meridian Creek—adventures for another day. Descend on switchbacks into the Douglas fir parkland of Toolbox Creek and after 2 miles, reach trip's end. Total hike, about 10 miles. Use the bike to go mostly downhill just over 2 miles to your car at Horse Creek.

Western Pioneer Mountains

59 PIONEER CABIN AND BEYOND

Best for: hiking
7.6 miles round trip
Moderate to strenuous
Elevation gain: 2,520 feet
High point: 9,480 feet
Hikable: mid-June through October
Map: USGS Hyndman Peak

From the southern Idaho prairies, travelers approaching the Wood River Valley see a series of white beacons rising north above the arid flatlands. The beacons are Hyndman Peak, Old Hyndman, and Cobb Peak in the Pioneer Mountains. Skiers on Sun Valley's Bald Mountain see these same summits fill their eastern horizon. A hike to Pioneer Cabin brings the Pioneer peaks almost to your boot toes. Almost 3,000 people a year (a virtual stampede by Idaho standards) labor up the 3.8-mile trail which gains 2,520 feet to the ridge just above the cabin—a good workout. While solitude may be missing unless you venture farther beyond, alpine scenery and wildflowers are not.

From Ketchum's one stoplight, drive north, past Sun Valley's one stoplight, on Trail Creek Road 408 and continue to Corral Creek Road 137 at 5 miles. Look up Corral Creek to see the tiptops of the three Pioneer landmarks: Duncan Ridge to the left, Hyndman Peak to its immediate right, and Cobb Peak farther south. Go 3.8 miles on dirt and gravel road to the trailhead.

(Corral Creek Road is used for springtime walks; a large avalanche annually blocks the canyon until May. The road is also mountain biked, but bikes are strongly discouraged on the Pioneer Cabin trail.)

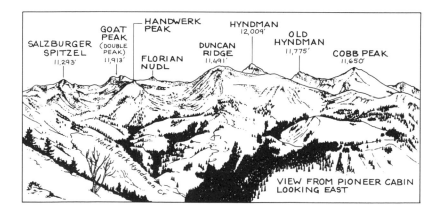

Cobb Peak (right) and Old Hyndman (left) from Pioneer Cabin

Cross Corral Creek to the trail register and embark on the upward climb, first along the stream, then through forest leading to the ridge and wide-open views at 2 miles. At 2.5 miles, pass a sign for Johnstone Creek trail leading to the East Fork of the Big Wood River. At this point you've managed a 1,880-foot elevation gain. Continue up the ridge for the next mile in full sun, gaining another 600 feet to the saddle just above the cabin. Summers are hot—bring water and remember the sunscreen and hat. If you have a dog along, pack extra water since there are no streams past the first mile. And be watchful of approaching storms which frequently scoot across the Pioneer Range.

Pioneer Cabin was built for ski tourers in 1937 and is still used by hikers and skiers. Today much of the country seen from Pioneer Cabin is included in the proposed Pioneer Mountain Wilderness, though the cabin itself is not.

The large drainage below Pioneer Cabin is the North Fork of Hyndman Creek. Its trail and several other routes to Pioneer Cabin are described in other guides listed in Further Reading in the Appendices.

For off-trail travelers Pioneer Cabin is just a beginning. Kane Lake lies below Salzburger Spitzel to the northeast; the Wildhorse Lakes are behind Goat Peak and Duncan Ridge. Most hikers will be content to picnic near the cabin's weathered boards and use binoculars or spotting scope to look for mountain goats in the tundra pastures. Watch, too, for a predator of goat kids, the golden eagle.

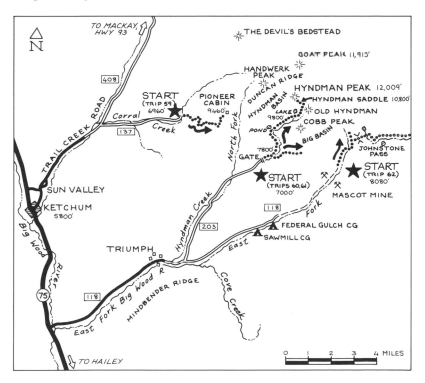

60 BIG BASIN

Best for: hiking
10 miles round trip
Strenuous
Elevation gain: 3,400 feet
High point: 10,400 feet
Hikable: mid-July through October
Maps: USGS Grays Peak, Hyndman Peak

Big Basin in the Pioneer Mountains lies south of Cobb Peak (11,650 feet). Like the mountain, which is rougher than a cob to climb, Big Basin has potential for gnarly moments, too. Go to Big Basin for inventive, arduous exploring, not for restful, horizontal walking or photographs of alpine lakes.

Plotting a course in Big Basin toward ridges reaching over 11,500 feet

From Ketchum, go south on Highway 75 for 5.5 miles to East Fork Road 118. Turn east and go 7 miles to Hyndman Creek Road 203. Turn left, continuing another 4.7 miles to a gate near the North Fork of Hyndman Creek. The 1985 gate ended debate on whether a stream ford was possible with four-wheel drive. Now a footbridge takes hikers safely across and the road beyond is closed to all motorized use.

The next few miles lead east, fully exposed to morning sun, uneventfully following the road toward the west face of Cobb. Nearing Cobb, roadway doldrums are nearly over. Flanking Cobb Peak are Hyndman Basin (trip 61) to the left (north) and Big Basin to the right (south). Watch for a fork in the road. Go right to turbulent Hyndman Creek, and search for a crossing. Wade if necessary (expect high water until midsummer).

Once across, a rough jeep trail climbs through the woods 1.5 miles to a mining claim high on a hillside. A horse trail leads up toward Big Basin, but meadows and bogs soon overrun it. There's no getting lost here. Stay on the ridge's center, continuing up and up. Now only time and energy will determine your response to Big Basin's call to adventure through plateaus of short grass, clear pools, clusters of purple gentians, ancient whitebark pines, and jumbles of rocks.

SAWTOOTH NATIONAL FOREST

61 HYNDMAN PEAK

Best for: hiking and scrambling
12.6 miles round trip
Strenuous
Elevation gain: 5,009 feet
High point: 12,009 feet
Hikable: mid-July through October
Maps: USGS Hyndman Peak, Grays Peak, Phi Kappa Mtn.,
    Standhope Peak

Turnaround at Hyndman Saddle
11 miles round trip
Strenuous
Elevation gain: 3,800 feet
High point: 10,800 feet

By a mere 9 feet, Hyndman achieves ranking in Idaho's 12,000-foot club. It's one of the few members not in the Lost River range. Another summit in the Pioneer Mountains comes close—Goat Peak at 11,913 feet. Mount Borah, at 12,662 feet, is the state's highest. But in Ketchum's backyard, Hyndman is the king. Local mountain folks like to climb the mountain, to stand over 12,000 feet high.

In climbing terms, Hyndman Peak is a "walk-up." However, teeter-totter skills are useful for ascending the peak's boulder field where wobbly rocks

Biking season along Hyndman Creek Road begins months before climbing season.

tremble under your weight. Stamina is helpful, too, for it's a 6-mile trip with a rigorous 5,009-foot elevation gain to the top. Also helpful—cross-country skills. After the first 2.5 miles there's no maintained trail and the path eventually vanishes. Try for a sunny day for your climb and begin ascending at daybreak—12,000 feet is not where to be in a lightning storm. And consider making this event a weekend outing and camping in Hyndman Basin.

The access directions are the same as for trip 60, Big Basin. As you approach Cobb Peak on the old road, stay left when the road forks and continue walking toward Cobb. As you near the base of the peak and see the creek, look for a trail going left by a boulder, up the hillside. Follow it, gaining 800 feet in 1 mile to a small pond which dries in late summer.

Cross a fork of Hyndman Creek and start climbing through Hyndman Basin. A packtrail fades in and out. The main branch of Hyndman Creek is on your right, below Cobb Peak. At 4.5 miles lies a small lake, sometimes called Hyndman Lake. Visit it on the return. Your immediate goal is Hyndman Saddle on the eastern skyline. The oddly bent mountain you see behind Cobb Peak is Old Hyndman; Duncan Ridge is northeast of Hyndman Peak.

At 5.5 miles, reach Hyndman Saddle. For most hikers this is reward enough. Hyndman Basin spreads stunningly below. Arrowhead Lake in wild Wildhorse Creek is southeast. But the view from the top is even grander. Go left on the 0.8-mile saddle-to-summit route and climb 1,209 feet up through the boulders. Tackling Hyndman requires more persistence than skill, but choose your steps with care. If dizziness or headache occur, turn back.

From atop Hyndman, look across the Pioneers and pick out Pioneer Cabin. Goat Peak is northward. In the far north, Castle Peak rises from the White Cloud Mountains. The Lost River Mountains are east. Skiers will recognize the runs of Bald Mountain where they've often looked toward Hyndman. Prairie lands stretch south. For help identifying the Pioneer topography you'll need four USGS quadrangles (Hyndman Peak sprawls over the corners of four maps).

SAWTOOTH NATIONAL FOREST

62 EAST FORK BIG WOOD RIVER HEADWATERS

> Best for: hiking
> 3 miles round trip (or longer)
> Easy to difficult
> Elevation gain: 1,000 feet (or more)
> High point: 9,000 feet
> Hikable: July to October
> Maps: USGS Hyndman Peak, Grays Peak

The upper East Fork Big Wood River canyon caused news in local papers in August 1984, when a cloudburst deluged the region, uprooting trees, sweep-

The Little Matterhorn in the upper East Fork Big Wood River

ing boulders downstream, and cutting gaping gullies. Campers at Federal Gulch were stranded, but unharmed. The switchback trail to Johnstone Pass was nearly obliterated. For hikers seeing the aftermath in the East Fork headwaters, darkening clouds give notice to pick safe campsites. With the passing of time, flood-damaged trails are being redefined, including a 1.5-mile path departing from the end of the rough East Fork Road. Because the access road goes far into the Pioneer Mountains, families will find alpine scenery at their car-door handle. But expect no lake or fishing stream.

From Ketchum, go south on Highway 75 for 5.5 miles to East Fork Road 118, turn east and continue 15 miles on two-wheel-drive road to the Mascot Mine. The next 1.6 miles to road's end are extremely rough; high clearance is needed. The present trail begins left of the creek, not to the right as shown on the 1967 Grays Peak topo. Wind through a rockslide and walk along the stream—a few sandy areas could accommodate a tent on a clear night.

Farther up canyon, farther than most small children will want to walk, the path crosses the rushing creek. There are large boulders on which to cross the creek, but wet boots can still be expected. At 1.5 miles, near a deep gully, a tattered sign (unless replaced) points southward up the damaged, but passable, foot trail toward Johnstone Pass, 10,000 feet high and 1.7 miles away. Beyond the pass lies Box canyon and Box canyon lakes. (Johnstone Pass is many miles from Johnstone Creek—a tributary to Hyndman Creek farther west in the Pioneers.)

Past the Johnstone turnoff, the East Fork drainage becomes increasingly a krummholz—alpine battlezone with bent and stunted trees. Flat spots are fewer and fewer; when one is found, declare a picnic break among the pink mountain heather. A look down the East Fork shows Grays Peak, an enormous, beautiful mountain to the south. An upper canyon landmark that author Clarice Blechmann called the "Little Matterhorn" towers above the north wall. A waterfall spills from snowfields, ice clings in the shadows. For high-line adventurers, there's an 11,000-foot skyline rim to the east; the headwaters of Wildhorse Creek are beyond.

SAWTOOTH NATIONAL FOREST

63 THE NARROWS

> Best for: mountain biking and hiking
> Opportunities for: scenic drive
> Ridable and Hikable: May through October
> Maps: USGS Baugh Creek SW, Hyndman Peak

Cove Creek to The Narrows Ride

> 8.8 miles round trip
> Easy
> Elevation gain: 350 feet
> High point: 6,520 feet

A round-trip walk to The Narrows can be short—a mile—or 2 miles or more. The 4-mile-long, fine-gravel and dirt surface of Cove Creek Road is well suited to mountain biking, so here's a chance to combine pedaling with hiking.

From Ketchum, drive 5.5 miles on Highway 75 to East Fork Road 118. Turn east, up the paved road, for nearly 6 miles to the old mining settlement of Triumph, passing along the way homes that are located to avoid the avalanche chutes of Mindbender Ridge. In the distance the Pioneer Mountains rise to the east, most notably the triangular, dished face of Cobb Peak.

Go past Triumph, traveling on rough washboard gravel and river rock along the East Fork of the Big Wood River, for 2.2 miles to Cove Creek Road 124 (don't expect a sign). Biking mileage begins here.

Go right on Cove Creek (south) through fenced pasturelands and start a gentle, but steady climb through the sage, aspen, and conifer of the canyon for the next 3.5 miles to a culvert and beaver ponds at Big Witch Creek (signless, but a side road leads left to sheep corrals). If you're driving, high clearance is required to go farther, and stream overflow in springtime makes the wheel-rutted meadows ahead impassable to vehicles. Please don't add further to the damage. (From here it's just over 0.5 mile to The Narrows trail.)

At 3.6 miles take the left road fork, crossing Moran Creek (a logging road goes right, up Moran Creek, to a locked gate). Watch at 4.1 miles for a faint trail going left, crossing Cabin Creek. The bluffs above The Narrows are ahead to the left. Hiking mileage begins here. (Cove Creek Road goes right, and continues over hill and dale to eventually join Quigley Creek canyon road from Hailey.)

The Narrows Hike

> 1 to 2 miles round trip
> Easy to moderate
> Elevation gain: 280 feet
> High point: 6,800 feet

Follow directions above to Cabin Creek. If driving rather than biking, and the roadbed is soggy, stop at Big Witch Creek and walk the last 0.6 mile to The Narrows trail. Cross small Cabin Creek by leaping its banks. The Narrows

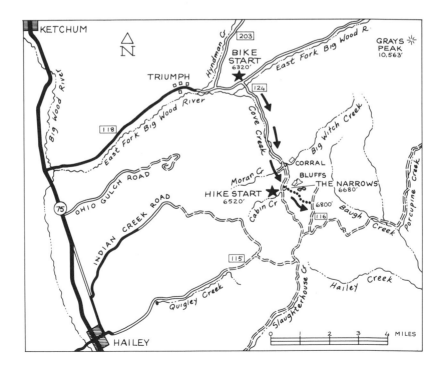

Exploring The Narrows

trail curves through thickets for 0.3 mile before reaching a wooden stockguard. Mountain bikers could ride this far, but the hill ahead is nearly impossible for wheels. For the next 150 yards, the path climbs a steep, bouldery slope to a jutting outcropping above The Narrows.

Scramble up the lichen-covered rocks for a gawk at the beaver network below. Overhead, watch for red-tailed hawks. Descend into the basin, 0.5 mile from Cove Creek Road. Stop here for a picnic on the grass, or explore the surrounding web of secret draws, aspen pockets, deer trails, and easily-scrambled knolls and points.

A hiking path continues from the basin, crosses two small streams, and climbs a long 0.5 mile to the east ridge, where it meets primitive road 116. Cross the road and hike 30 yards to the hilltop and look into Baugh Creek and southeast to the Little Wood River region. Grays Peak (10,563 feet) is northeast, a startling giant of a mountain, especially when snow covered. By mid-May the arid sage landscape above The Narrows bursts with colorful wildflowers. Unless venturing off-trail, retrace your steps back to The Narrows. (Hilly road 116 goes south toward routes leading either to Baugh Creek, Quigley Canyon, or, via tumultuous ups and downs, back to Cove Creek.)

■ Appendices ■

Trip Matrix

Choose an activity and a locale. Outings with shorter or easier segments may have one or more ratings. The access road to the trip's departure point is listed as paved; two-wheel drive gravel or dirt road; and four-wheel drive or high-clearance primitive road. Backpacking and car camping opportunities are noted along with trips that have historical sights. Some access roads to hiker trailheads, as well as bike trips or segments of bike trips, are suitable for scenic drives. Read the full trip descriptions for more information.

	Hiking				Mountain Biking			Access Road			Camping		Other	
	Easy	Moderate	Difficult	Strenuous	Easy	Moderate	Difficult	Paved	Two-WD Gravel or Dirt	Four-WD or High Clearance	Backpacking	Car Camping	Historical Sites	Scenic Drive Segments
STANLEY AND SALMON RIVER MOUNTAINS														
1. Rookie Point		•							•				•	•
2. Custer Motorway		•			•	•	•		•				•	•
3. Bayhorse, Bayhorse Lakes	•	•				•			•				•	•
4. Loon Creek, Beaver Creek Road		•				•	•			•	•	•	•	•
5. Nip and Tuck					•	•			•				•	•
6. East Fork Nip and Tuck Creek	•	•							•					
7. Joe's Gulch		•				•	•		•				•	
8. Basin Creek	•					•		•				•		
9. Noho Trail						•		•						
10. Basin Butte Lookout					•	•	•		•					•
11. Hindman Lake, Cabin Creek Peak		•					•			•	•	•		•
12. Blind Summit					•	•			•					•
13. Valley Creek, Knapp Creek						•			•					
14. Marsh Creek, Big Hole, Dagger Falls	•	•							•		•	•		•
SAWTOOTH MOUNTAINS														
Northern Sawtooths														
15. Iron Creek, Sawtooth Lake	•	•							•		•			
16. Elk Mountain, Elk Meadow					•	•			•			•		•

Autumn colors on Horton Peak aspen groves

	Hiking				Mountain Biking			Access Road			Camping		Other	
	Easy	Moderate	Difficult	Strenuous	Easy	Moderate	Difficult	Paved	Two-WD Gravel or Dirt	Four-WD or High Clearance	Backpacking	Car Camping	Historical Sites	Scenic Drive Segments
17. Lady Face and Bridal Veil Falls	•	•							•		•			
18. Observation Peak				•					•		•			
Redfish Lake														
19. Redfish Lake Walks	•				•				•			•	•	•
20. Redfish Trailhead Classic Hike I: Bench Lakes		•							•					
21. Redfish Trailhead Classic Hike II: Fishhook Creek Meadow	•								•					
Redfish Lake Inlet														
22. Lily Lake, Redfish Lake Creek Falls	•								•					
23. Grand Mogul Trail	•	•							•			•		
24. Garden of Giants, Flat Rock Junction		•							•			•		
25. Elephant's Perch, Saddleback Lakes			•						•			•		
26. Alpine Lake, Baron Divide		•		•					•			•		
27. Cramer Lakes, The Temple, Cramer Divide				•					•			•		
Hell Roaring														
28. Hell Roaring Creek Pond	•								•		•			
29. Hell Roaring Lake, Finger of Fate	•									•	•			
30. Imogene Lake, Imogene Divide		•		•						•	•			
Pettit Lake														
31. Pettit Lake Hikes	•	•							•			•		
32. Yellow Belly Lake	•					•			•			•		•
33. Alice Lake, Snowyside Pass	•	•		•					•		•			
34. Toxaway Canyon Hikes		•		•					•		•			
Alturas Lake														
35. Alturas Lake Creek					•				•				•	•
36. Alturas Lake to Pettit Lake Loop					•	•			•			•		
37. Alturas Lake South Shore	•								•			•		
38. Alpine Creek Knoll	•	•								•	•			
39. Mattingly Creek			•							•	•			
40. Cabin Creek Lakes		•								•	•			
Upper Sawtooth Valley														
41. Sawtooth City					•				•			•	•	•
42. Smiley Creek Canyon, Vienna	•						•		•	•		•	•	•
43. Galena Wagon Road					•	•			•	•		•	•	•
44. Frenchman Creek					•	•			•	•		•		•
45. Pole Creek					•	•			•	•			•	•
46. Valley Road, Horton Peak			•		•				•			•		•

	Hiking				Mountain Biking			Access Road			Camping		Other	
	Easy	Moderate	Difficult	Strenuous	Easy	Moderate	Difficult	Paved	Two-WD Gravel or Dirt	Four-WD or High Clearance	Backpacking	Car Camping	Historical Sites	Scenic Drive Segments
WHITE CLOUD MOUNTAINS														
47. Rough Creek, Lookout Mountain	•			•					•		•			
48. Jimmy Smith Lake	•							•	•					•
49. Heart Lake, Six Lakes Basin		•	•						•		•			
50. Fourth of July Lake, Blackman Peak	•	•							•		•			
51. Washington Peak		•		•						•			•	•
52. Castle Divide, Castle Peak				•						•	•			
GALENA TO PIONEER MOUNTAINS														
Smoky Mountains														
53. Baker Creek and Prairie Creek Lakes	•	•							•		•	•		•
54. Lost Shirt Gulch		•		•					•					
55. Ketchum Fat-tire Classic: Adams Gulch						•			•					
Boulder Mountains														
56. North Fork Big Wood River Hikes	•	•							•		•	•		•
57. Hunter Creek Summit		•								•	•	•		
58. Herd Peak			•						•			•		
Western Pioneer Mountains														
59. Pioneer Cabin and Beyond		•							•		•			
60. Big Basin			•						•		•			
61. Hyndman Peak			•						•		•			
62. East Fork Big Wood River Headwaters	•		•							•	•			•
63. The Narrows	•				•				•					•

Short Hikes

These destinations (or the portion listed in parentheses) are suggested for families and senior hikers. Read the trip descriptions for further information.

	Round-trip distances		
	Up to 1 mile	1-3 miles	Over 3 miles
STANLEY AND SALMON RIVER MOUNTAINS			
3. Bayhorse Lakes		•	
6. East Fork Nip and Tuck Creek		•	

	Round-trip distances		
	Up to 1 mile	1-3 miles	Over 3 miles
14. Marsh Creek, Big Hole (Marsh Creek trail)		•	•

SAWTOOTHS

15. Iron Creek, Sawtooth Lake (Iron Creek Meadow)		•	•
16. Elk Mountain, Elk Meadow		•	
17. Lady Face and Bridal Veil Falls		•	•
19. Redfish Lake Walks	•		
20. Redfish Trailhead Classic Hike I: Bench Lakes			•
21. Redfish Trailhead Classic Hike II: Fishhook Creek Meadow		•	
22. Lily Lake, Redfish Lake Creek Falls	•	•	
23. Grand Mogul		•	
24. Garden of Giants, Flat Rock Junction		•	•
28. Hell Roaring Creek Pond		•	•
29. Hell Roaring Lake			•
31. Pettit Lake Hikes		•	
32. Yellow Belly Lake	•	•	
33. Alice Lake ("Halfway Pond")			•
34. Toxaway Canyon Hikes (Farley Lake)			•
37. Alturas Lake South Shore	•	•	•
38. Alpine Creek Knoll		•	
40. Cabin Creek Lakes			•
42. Smiley Creek Canyon, Vienna	•		

WHITE CLOUD MOUNTAINS

47. Rough Creek, Lookout Mountain (Rough Creek Trail)		•	
48. Jimmy Smith Lake		•	
49. Heart Lake		•	
50. Fourth of July Lake		•	•

SMOKY MOUNTAINS

53. Baker Creek and Prairie Creek Lakes (Baker Lake and Mill Lake)		•	•

BOULDER MOUNTAINS

56. North Fork Big Wood River Hikes (North Fork and West Fork trails)		•	•

Easy Mountain Bike Rides

These rides are suggested for families or seniors. The trip sections in parentheses are shorter or easier portions of a longer ride. See the text for matching miles to your pedalling power.

Sources of Information

CHAMBERS OF COMMERCE

Sun Valley/Ketchum
  Chamber of Commerce
Box 2420
Sun Valley, ID 83353
(208) 726-3423
(800) 634-3347

Stanley-Sawtooth
  Chamber of Commerce
Box 59
Stanley, ID 83278
(208) 774-3411

Challis Chamber of Commerce
Box 1130
Challis, ID 83226
(208) 879-2771

FORESTRY OFFICES

Forest Supervisor
Sawtooth National Forest
2675 Kimberly Road East
Twin Falls, ID 83301
(208) 737-3200

Forest Supervisor
Salmon/Challis National Forest
Box 729
Salmon, ID 83467
(208) 765-2215

Sawtooth National Recreation Area
Star Route
Ketchum, ID 83340
(208) 726-7672

Lost River Ranger District
Box 507
Mackay, ID 83251
(208) 588-2224

Stanley Ranger Station
Stanley, ID 83278
(208) 774-3681

Yankee Fork Ranger District
HC 67, Box 650
Clayton, ID 83227
(208) 838-2201

Ketchum Ranger District
Box 2356
Ketchum, ID 83340
(208) 622-5371

IDAHO DEPARTMENT OF FISH & GAME, DISTRICT OFFICES

Idaho Department of Fish & Game
Jerome, ID 83338
(Ketchum area, Big Wood River
   drainage)
(208) 423-4359

Idaho Department of Fish & Game
Salmon, ID 83467
(Stanley area, Salmon River
   drainage)
(208) 756-2271

Idaho Department of Fish & Game
1515 Lincoln Road
Idaho Falls, ID 83401
(Mackay, Big Lost River drainage)
(208) 522-7783

IDAHO OUTFITTERS AND GUIDES

Idaho Outfitters & Guides
   Association
Box 95
Boise, ID 83701
(208) 342-1438

CONSERVATION ORGANIZATIONS

Idaho Conservation League
Wood River Chapter
Box 2671
Ketchum, ID 83340
(208) 726-8437
(208) 726-7485

The Wilderness Society
413 West Idaho Street, Suite 102
Boise, ID 83702
(208) 343-8153

Idaho Conservation League
Box 844
Boise, ID 83701
(208) 345-6933

Sierra Club
Northern Rockies Chapter
Box 1173
Pocatello, ID 83204

Boulder-White Clouds Council
Box 653
Boise, ID 83701
(208) 345-9067
(208) 726-1065

Further Reading

BACKPACKING ONE STEP AT A TIME, by Harvey Manning (Vintage Books, 1972). An entertaining handbook for making the transition from sidewalk to wilderness trails.

SOFT PATHS, by Bruce Hampton and David Cole, The National Outdoor Leadership School (Stackpole Books, 1988). Gives state-of-the-art information on low-impact skills for enjoying the wilderness without harming it.

DAY HIKING NEAR SUN VALLEY, by Anne Hollingshead and Gloria Moore (Gentian Press, 1987). Covers 80 hiking trails, including several routes to Pioneer Cabin, and provides wildflower lists.

THE HIKER'S GUIDE TO IDAHO, by Jackie Johnson Maughan (Falcon Press, 1989). A statewide day-hiking and backpacking guide to 80 trips, many in proposed-wilderness areas, including the Lemhi Range and Lost River Mountains. Also features a dozen trips in the Frank Church–River of No Return Wilderness.

TRAILS OF THE SAWTOOTH AND WHITE CLOUD MOUNTAINS, by Margaret Fuller (Signpost Books, 1988). The most comprehensive guide for extended backpacking or horsepacking trips into the Sawtooths and White Clouds, covering nearly every trail. Includes portions of the Sawtooth Wilderness approached via the Boise National Forest on the south side of the range.

TRAILS OF THE FRANK CHURCH–RIVER OF NO RETURN WILDERNESS, by Margaret Fuller (Signpost Books, 1987). Provides trail information and glimpses of history for this vast 2.3-million-acre wilderness, the largest in the continental United States.

■ Index ■

Author Lynne Stone

About the Author: Lynne Stone grew up on a wheat ranch near Condon, Oregon. As a resident of Ketchum since 1981, Stone has been involved in the struggle to designate more Idaho lands as wilderness. She once brought a dead wolverine (on ice) to a Congressional field hearing in Boise to bring attention to the threatened species and its endangered habitat. After a decade in the ski retail business, Stone turned to writing and conservation work to encourage people to visit and become advocates for preserving wilderness areas. She works for the Boulder-White Clouds Council, an environmental group focusing on public lands issues in central Idaho.